CREATIVITY IS EVERYTHING

TORRON-LEE DEWAR

ISBN 978-1545549339

CONTENTS

ACKNOWLEDGEMENTS

I would like to thank:

Family, close friends and level-headed acquaintances for being there to support my daily struggles, and successes.

Those who have given me inspiration and motivation to prevail over life's toughest challenges.

INTRODUCTION

In each new day of our lives, we continuously wonder if we are making the right choices. We ask ourselves if this is the way we should be living and often find ourselves dreaming of a better tomorrow. In this day and age, it's hard not to become gloomy due to all of life's aggressive demands. We must remember that we are only human... not machines. We are human for a reason, and therefore, shouldn't always be so hard on ourselves.

The main purpose of this book is to open your mindset to a higher level of elevated thinking, which you can apply to your daily lifestyle. Freeing the mind is a lot easier than most people initially anticipate.

Being optimistic makes us feel better about ourselves, whilst being pessimistic makes us feel broken and dull. You don't get paid to hate or be miserable, so why work for free? This is where some people will say, "You don't get paid to be happy either" but that's incorrect. Happiness rewards you greatly, whereas negativity punishes you greatly. Bad thoughts lead to stress, which in turn can often lead to illness in the long term. Ask yourself, is it worth it?

We were put on this planet to live openly and freely, whether that be exploring, learning new things, or just being content with ourselves. We were not made to constantly doubt ourselves and sit in a corner for the rest of our lives.

The first step to self-improvement is allowing someone else to show us how, and you've passed this step just by reading this page! Having this very book in your hands can only mean one thing; you're willing to find out how to improve your positive charisma and feel refreshed on an everyday basis. Who doesn't want that?

Being open-minded allows us to upgrade ourselves, sometimes in ways we never thought were possible. No one is perfect, and we all have areas which we could brush up on. Ultimately, knowledge is power.

We are surrounded by negativity most days throughout the overall course of our lives, which is why it's important to think about the positives and create stability. I believe that a healthy mind leads to a healthy life. Being angry or adopting a defeatist outlook all the time leads to stress, and we all know what stress does to the body. Imagine what type of person you could be if you saw through the negative illusions in life and focused on the positives.

Day-to-day living becomes much more exciting and pleasant when you're the one in control. There will always be situations that appear out of nowhere, ploughing into us without warning. We might not always be able to see fate coming, but we can respond to these discrepancies in a way that leaves us feeling empowered.

Hopefully, after reading this book, you will find inspiration in some form that will change the way you view the world we live in!

1

PREMONITION

We often live our entire life based on a prediction of how we think we should be living. For example, you might've been brought up in a rough area and automatically think you should be living a hard life based on crime and mindless decisions. Or maybe your parents are wealthy and expected you to go to university, so you live your life based on what society expects you to do. People, in general, don't like it when others are different. People don't know how to process unique individuality because we are brainwashed into a one-track mindset without even knowing it. Our lives gradually become a default template that we're automatically expected to follow with no real question as to why.

It's great if you have people around to steer you in the right direction, but if you don't, that's also okay because you can be your own navigation in the world we live in. Sometimes you have to be your own beacon of light because when people don't believe in you, you must believe in yourself. Most of the time, those around us want to see us thrive and do well, and that's mainly the reason behind them pushing to make our decisions for us. However, if that goes too far, you'll spend endless years wishing you had done something differently. It's far better to have an interest in the aim in the first place. Having an interest in what it is you're trying to achieve makes your life a lot more pleasant.

The main root of negativity often comes from people being terribly unhappy with what they do for a living. Of course, certain issues might make life a lot harder than it has to be, and that's understandable. However, it's all too common to make the classic mistake of being ignorant just because you think you've got it covered. Your excuses for not living a happy life might be fully justifiable, but not even bothering to make a change in your life simply isn't.

Everyone has something they like or are skilled at. You might not realise it yet, or maybe don't believe you are, but everyone gets a buzz from doing something. Only you will know what that something is, and once you discover it, you'll instantly know that you wouldn't mind doing it for most of your years because it brings you peace or makes you feel good.

You say, "What I like doing won't make me money." That's true, and perhaps it won't. However, you shouldn't restrict yourself from life's little pleasures. Doing the things that give us a positive buzz motivates us in the duller aspects of our lives and somehow, we work out how to fill in the grey areas. Ask yourself, what were people doing before the currency system existed? Our generation is so fixed on only the financial side of society, but ask yourself, how can you even generate an income if you don't have the correct mindset anyway?

For a second, just forget money even exists. You don't need money to breathe, feel satisfied or kick-start creativity. Money doesn't create happiness; we just think it does from the constant images we see on a daily basis. We wake up, and before even opening the curtains to allow light into our homes, we reach for our mobile phones to have a scroll through mindless news that mostly doesn't concern or uplift us. So already the day is off to a bad start. Then, we stumble across the room before making any breakfast and turn on the TV, only to see celebrities living their lives and think, "That looks good... why aren't I doing that?" After a few more flicks of the remote, we end up on the news channel to pollute our minds of all the wrong in our world.

Even after we're up and about, we go for a walk and see others in extremely wealthy positions and think they deserve more respect than us. No person is greater than you, and you are no greater than anyone else. We are equal. Keep this in mind the next time you feel inferior for any reason.

It's totally pointless going through life doing things you absolutely hate for the sole reason of impressing someone else. That would make you a fool. For us to truly become a master at something, we must first dedicate ourselves to the thing we love the most until we are professionals in that field. How do you expect to become good at something if you never stick at it in the first place? How do you expect to excel in what you love if you never make time for what you love? Ignorance leads us to the same old conclusion: I don't have what it takes to become the person I want to be, or I doubt it'll make enough money to pay the bills.

If you focus on your vision, you'll have no trouble in becoming happy. You never know, you might also end up making money from it. But don't make everything revolve around finance or you'll never be satis-fied. Try engaging in things just because you want to. Don't always second guess your happiness and find reasons not to delve into what you enjoy.

To be starkly honest, there are only two options really. Live unhap-pily, pay bills and moan for the rest of your life, or do the things you enjoy, raise your general confidence in being a human, and use the world to your advantage. Doing 50% of what you enjoy is better than doing 100% of what you hate... sounds appealing right?

The only person stopping you from being who you want to be is you. When sitting for a moment to take everything in, you realise that anything in existence can be reached. It all falls down to whether or not you're going to take the first step. We base ourselves below the standard we think has already been set. In other words, we continuously tell our mind that if someone is really good at what they do, we cannot achieve the same standard if not better. A lot of us have great aspirations but always limit ourselves as to what we can truly achieve.

The next time you go to second guess yourself, just remember that your role models do not doubt themselves. They might question certain areas of their own lives, but if they were to keep doing that, then how would they have gone forth to inspire you in the first place? Clearly, they overcame this mental barrier and learned to see that it doesn't exist.

When you think about your inspiration, don't say, "I can't do it because they are already too good at it." Do you think they say the same about other people? Do the people you aspire to be like wake up and think, "Oh, they're already legendary at that, I better not challenge myself?" It's unlikely. They get on with chasing what they want out of life and that's all there is to it. You should have the same mindset as a unique being. Adopt your new aura of creativity and leap beyond the constraints of your premade stereotype.

We must work up to things in a gradual motion, even when we want something right away that is out of reach. Everything has a process, and it's good to build in stages. Most successful people will rarely ever show you the procedure... just the end result, so don't be fooled.

Try not to waste energy worrying if others get you. As long as you get yourself, that's all that matters. Self-acceptance is the gateway to progression.

Be mindful of what you talk about. Some things can be spoken straight into existence.

TORRON-LEE DEWAR

2

BECOME OPEN-MINDED

Appreciate every moment in life, and the good people you come across. We can always learn something from someone; so try not to be ignorant because it'll hold you back in life. You will only get these minutes once in your life, in this current scenario, so make the most of the energy.

At times, certain individuals might try to converse with you, and you don't fully take in what they're saying because you don't associate yourself to be like them. By doing this, you throw away a ton of energy that could've been beneficial to your life, like the missing piece of a puzzle. Give people a chance; you never know... you might be surprised by what information they have to offer. If someone's words are negative, however, you have learned not to listen to them again. The information we choose to accept is always optional.

You're the boss of how people can make you feel. If you don't give someone permission to make you feel inferior, then they can't. If we keep entertaining someone's negative energies toward us, they will continue to carry on with their destructive trail of cynicism. This is where body language comes into the equation. Usually, if the person you communicate with has caught your interest, you may notice that your body naturally tends to face them in a relaxed manner. If you sense hostility in a conversation you wish to exit, then the opposite should be applied with a more disengaged stance, letting the person know you don't plan on sticking around. In the long run, those who try to put you down will soon absorb the message that you don't plan on being anyone's doormat and eventually back down from being condescending. Body language can help us unlock the most out of someone's soul. By showing the speaker that they have your complete attention, you may find that they are willing to open up about themselves further and hold a much deeper, spiritually connected conversation.

Learning to control your kinesics effectively will take you a long way when it comes to learning from others. We are always growing and building upon what we already know. As a building sits over time, it becomes unstable. Scaffolding is erected and the structure is rejuvenated. You should be upgrading in the same way as you go through life. The long-abandoned structure that doesn't see the scaffolding will collapse and the same goes for us humans in regard to being open-minded. Try to take something away from every situation and learn from it to become wiser. There is never any bad that comes of being wiser.

How you choose to live your life is down to your personal preference. Religion, social status, or our surroundings have nothing to do with it. You make your own decisions every day, and it's easy for us to hide behind pathetic excuses. Sometimes we find ourselves doing things for long periods of time and never stop for a second to think about what we are actually doing. Don't forget that you've got one opportunity to live a meaningful lifestyle suited to you. If you can't create your own identity and be passionate about the things you love in this lifetime, then when can you?

Experiment with things that improve your life and make you feel satisfied, whether it be in terms of work, fashion, or engaging hobbies.

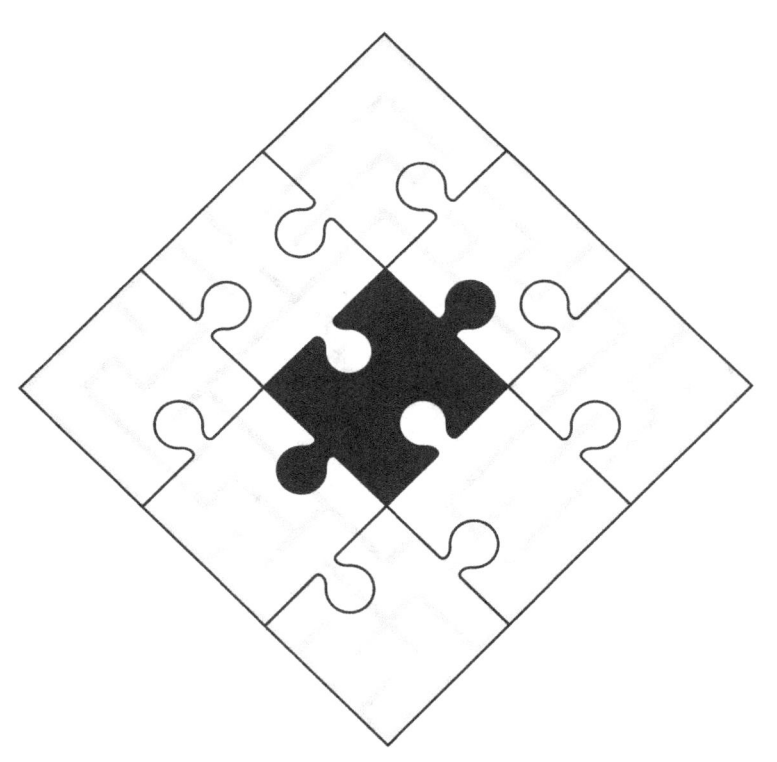

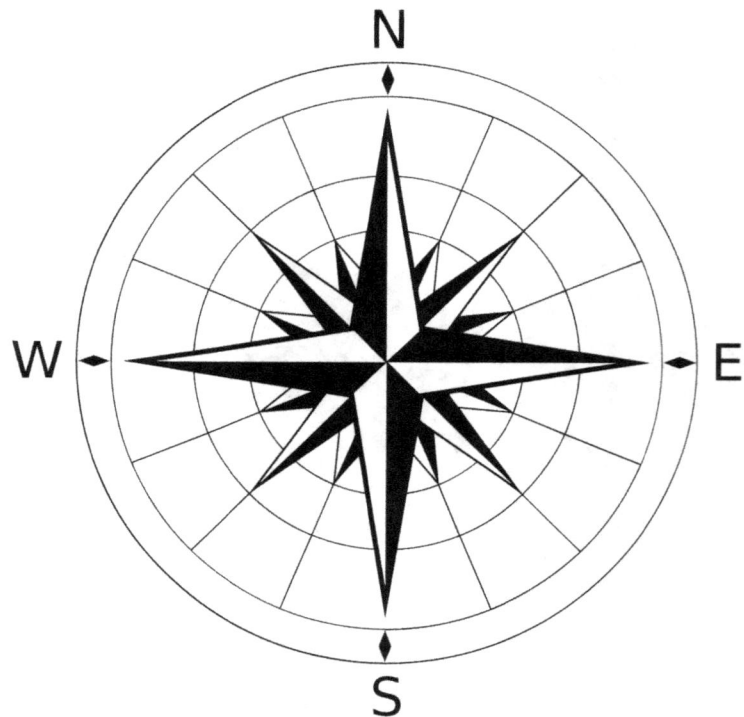

3

IMPROVISE AND ADAPT TO CHANGES

It's easy to get wrapped up in our own comfort zones from time to time, and when change comes, we don't really know how to process it. You might be placed in a situation that is completely new to you or feel like you don't have the courage to endure what's up ahead. To conquer this mental barrier, we must absorb our surroundings and find little things that inspire us to move forth. Remember, tiny outlets of optimism can be found in even the most unlikely places, and we must use these outlets to reach the light at the end of the tunnel. This concept always stuck with me when I witnessed how people in other countries made do with what they had.

When thrown into a hole of uncertainty, tools must be crafted in order to navigate our way out. These tools are crafted by learning to accept our current situations, and by finding ways in which we cannot only inspire but also feel good within. At times like this, we often learn about who we are and what we can attain from that moment forward.

Every so often, we can be caught off guard, and believe me, it really does happen to the best of us. Some days we're as confident as ever, and other days we feel completely bewildered or anxious about something.

It's how you respond to these events that plays a huge part in our own self-discovery. Personally, I always admired the way my mother managed to overcome and adapt to certain changes as we grew up... combatting pessimism with a profound sense of resourcefulness.

At specific stages of your life, you will reach a crossroads. And usually, the only two options are to give up or carry on. Limited options are always daunting, however, with time and dedication, your newly established mindset will be able to make these decisions effectively. Nothing in life is perfect, so flaws should always be celebrated where possible. Accepting the idea that little blips may appear on your map will free up a greater amount of headspace in the long run.

Understanding that nothing is promised, and nothing is permanent can be a great way to overcome the sudden challenges that pop up on our journey. Once this newly crafted mindset of yours is in motion, everything should just flow a lot more freely. Even once the wheels of confidence and self-belief start turning, we shall continue to add pieces of coal to the fire. These pieces of coal symbolise positivity, faith, and commitment to one's self as a person.

Have heart in the things you do. You don't always need a second or third opinion for every last decision you make. If we ponder too much on the opinion of others, we may never get to the end goal. Imagine waiting all your life to do something and because you're presented with a challenge, you give up and go off in the other direction. That's not what life is about. If you do this frequently, it's time to change this mentality. The spiteful things people say can easily make us change course fast because we can't bear the thought of being looked down on. Not showing a single care and carrying on is where it's at! Letting people know you don't give a damn is an attractive trait to show off.

The human soul is hindered when too much thought is spent being overly conscious about how others perceive you. All of this non-stop energy is sucked down a plug hole and isn't directed to anywhere useful. It could be compared to harvesting ripe fruits from a tree only to toss them onto the floor. No one benefits from these actions.

Altering your course of direction is completely acceptable. You might enjoy cricket this year and in four years time, want to take up rowing. Baking could be your thing now and later, gardening. The possibilities of combinations are absolutely limitless. People rarely stick to a single path for their entire life, and your calling could unquestionably consist of a mixture of things. The problem is, we're dying to fit in too badly. And the question is, why? Our sense of individuality seems to vanish past a certain point in our lives. We then begin to invest too much energy dwelling on what others think of our aesthetic. But in the end, no one ever truly gets further afield by fitting in.

You're not supposed to stop in a pitch dark forest when running through the unknown. Life is no different in that regard, so we must keep moving and maintain the momentum. Whether we're sprinting or walking doesn't matter, so long as we're actually moving forward. Stopping dead in the darkness of society's tirade leaves us vulnerable to an ambush. Be fierce when it's necessary and light the atmosphere up. Clarity is gained when we defend ourselves. It gives us a huge surge of overall confidence. The type of confidence we need amid a bleak community.

When dealing with life's unknown, try not to be a shape that cannot adapt to certain atmospheres. But rather, like a stream as it moulds to its environment in order to find the best possible route to maintain its flow. This is the way in which we learn about ourselves and open up opportunities to be optimistic in life.

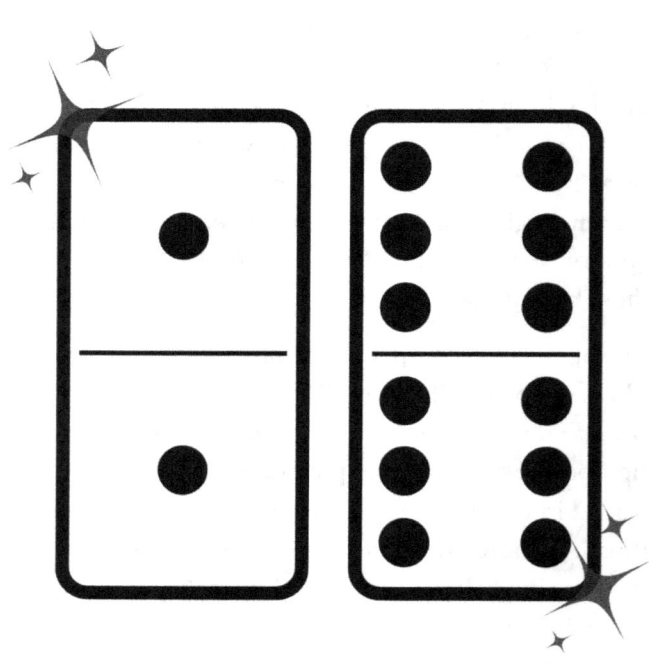

4

LEARN TO RESPECT YOURSELF

W e put ourselves down at times because of what someone else said to us. The sooner you learn to respect yourself, the sooner you can start living life.

Don't continuously seek approval from every Tom, Dick, and Harry that comes your way. Be polite but focused in a way that shows others you respect yourself. People will treat you with respect if you come across as open but mentally strong at the same time. It's not something you must constantly think about... it'll just become part of your persona after a while.

In doing so, we must remember to avoid transforming into a negative, over-opinionated person without realising, as this can easily happen without us knowing. If we spend too much time around spiteful, uneducated people, there's a strong chance that their personality might rub off onto us. It's so easy for the subconscious mind to start adopting traits from its environment, and if your atmosphere is made up of a mostly toxic surrounding, then the rest is pretty self-explanatory. When I was new to the world of entrepreneurial ventures, a gent named Grantley Yearwood was there to support my vision. At the time, he worked for the council's youth service and was also an aircraft engineer alongside being a magistrate. Regardless of his demanding schedule, time was always devoted to the project I had been working so hard on, and he encouraged me to respect my own values which further enabled me to attack challenges. The aim of the project was to bring others away from the street crime that plagued our urban environments. Our ethos, to prevent self-harm, depression, and other negative issues that were happening in the area through the power of the arts. I was extremely grateful for the opportunity and the project went on to be a success. This was a clear indication of how devoting time to others could be so crucial to improving the world we live in.

Usually, all it takes is one person to give faith, and from there, a snow-ball effect happens. When helping and giving back to others in the world, I like to reflect on this concept regularly. I like to think back on how the strength of self-belief isn't to be underestimated. There is something called the domino effect where the events of one situation can lead to many other events occurring later down the line. It's a sort of, "Reap what you sow" mentality where your deeds now will determine what goes on around you later on in life. It's a hugely relevant topic that is so often overlooked in the modern world, and perhaps, that's partly the reason why people make so many bad decisions.

Bad decisions are usually the consequences of the thought process being completely absent just before taking the leap. Allowing more time for the brain to analyse the situation tends to lead towards greater successes. For example, "If I use this thin rope to suspend myself over this cliff, will it snap easily resulting in my demise?" There is never any harm in sticking firmly to your beliefs in why you should do things a certain way, especially when you feel it benefits the greater good. So in a nutshell, giving someone else the best possible support you can give them at the time is far better than offering substandard support. Sure, any support is better than none, but if you want it to also benefit you as a person, then the former is a much better choice. Longevity is the key in pretty much all aspects of life.

All too often, I've been in situations where I felt as though others weren't taking me seriously. Sort of like I continuously had to prove my worth in order to be noticed by those harnessing the power to open doors. I quickly learnt that the strain of trying to impress others was a never-ending saga that wasn't beneficial to the soul. There would always be someone you couldn't impress. You could change up your image 100 times over, and again, there would still be someone who didn't approve of your character. All you're doing is wasting time chasing clout that doesn't even improve you as a person anyway. Learn to be comfortable in your own skin and get good at being the greatest version of yourself. That is the only way forward.

Imagine when you used paints for the first time... you mixed a little of one colour with another and it blended into a similar shade, whereas other colours that mixed seemed to create a totally new shade. You want to be the new shade of colour. The new shade is you learning and adapting to your own identity.

It's easy to go around seeking the approval of others over and over again, to the point where we forget we're even doing it! Breaking this unethical habit will ensure you get the best out of being yourself. And being yourself doesn't require any approval at all. There is absolutely no need to constantly seek validation from others. The world is magnetised to those that are sure of themselves, and even when you aren't sure of yourself, accepting who you are and doing the best for yourself is a healthy thing to do. Inner acceptance radiates.

Like anything in life, spending time around good things will eventually make us good, being around inspiring things leads to inspiration, and so on. Be the artist of your own picture and make it a masterpiece.

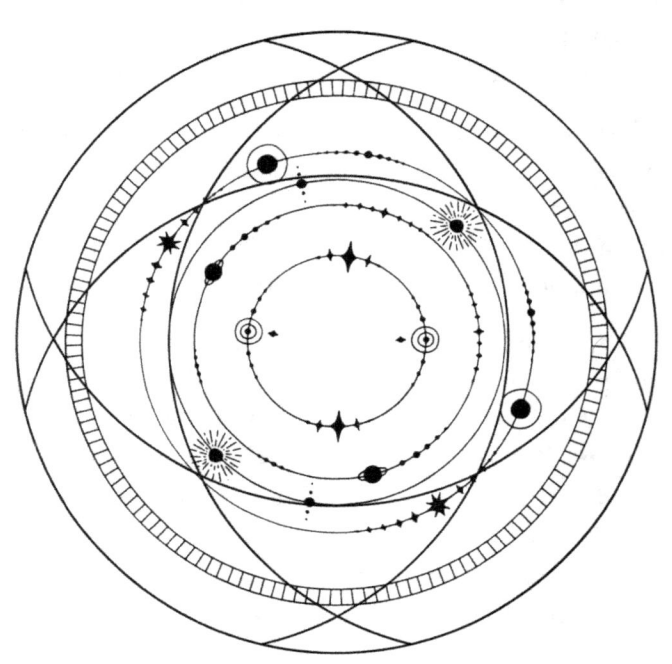

5

RELAX

F eeling relaxed is the first step to unlocking our greatest potential. Stress and hostility just lead us on a path of self-destruction. We all need to take a moment out of our bustling lives to sit back and appreciate our time on this planet. Think big... wonder more. As humans in the modern-day, we are so confined with our ideologies and way of thinking due to our education and work system.

Reflect on living in a small town, then remember that small town is in a borough, which in turn, is part of a vaster metropolis or county which belongs to a country. That country is one of many belonging to planet Earth, and Earth belongs to a solar system which is part of a larger galaxy. There are many other galaxies in our universe, and from that point, it's a mystery. Thinking in this expanded, larger-scale manner will enable you to be bolder when chasing opportunities. Becoming the most confident person you can possibly be whilst still remaining grounded and humble is the ultimate goal.

It's easy to take life for granted, so we must always reflect and remind ourselves that it could always be much worse. By thinking more freely, we start to appreciate our surroundings, relationships and everything in between that's been accomplished or done for us in the past. Take a few minutes each day if you remember, to just feel good for no apparent reason. If you can learn to do that, no one will be in charge of your contentment. Don't worry about things so much, as a lot of issues are out of our control anyway. There is no need to be overwhelmed by life. Breathe.

It's down to you how you choose to rest. However, it would be a wise choice to separate yourself from anything screen related from time to time. The TV screen, and most screens in general are usually where most of our problems stem from. Depressing dramas and senseless violence makes us unconsciously sick due to the repetition of mundane events. This cycle of woe is destructive and has no benefits.

We all need a rest from time to time, to remind ourselves that we are human. The things we see on a day-to-day basis and on the Internet are often misconceptions of the perfect life. Ultimately, life is what you make it. Meditation allows our brains to eliminate all of the junk being harnessed inside which makes us stressed. When doing so, the process brings us back to Earth thus increasing our self-awareness. Those who do not meditate or allow time to themselves tend to be in an artificial trance and lose their soul in modern-day society. Breaking this fabricated daze realigns our vision, levelling us in tune with the present, here... now.

During meditation, we become detached from the physical world and begin to see our lives from a more conscious perspective. It's so easy to get flustered in the chaos of life and even easier to completely lose all focus in the process. Ensuring enough time is taken out to balance your busy life will dissolve the bulk of your problems. Remember, most of people's stress is down to a lack of organisation and absence of discipline.

Meditation allows us to feel present and helps us visualise what we desire most whilst reinforcing purpose.

6

MEDITATION IS YOUR FRIEND

S o long as you're in a safe environment, you can meditate anywhere at any time to give yourself tranquillity no matter what's happening around you. A quieter atmosphere works best with minimal distractions. Different timescales work best for different individuals. However, starting with a simple 5 minutes here and there should help to build your meditation practice. Find out what works best for you and then simply build up from there.

Once you've decided how long you'd like to meditate for and at what time of the day, you can try to maintain the cycle so it becomes part of your daily routine. We don't always get the opportunity to do this, so any amount of meditation is better than none at all. Meditation first came onto my radar by talking to my local shopkeeper Mr. Aswin Patel. I'd walk round to the parade to collect my Nan's newspaper he would save and end up chatting about life, overcoming difficulties and becoming a better human. The qualities and outlooks Aswin harnessed were immensely inspiring.

Aswin, who we knew as "Adnam" explained how meditation helped him with certain aspects of his life and how he saw the world through different eyes since practising it. Kind of like being woken up from a trance that we aren't aware of being in. Even in tough times when he didn't put the heating on in the shop and would sit there happily in a thick jacket and woollen flat cap, he'd still have a warm smile on his face. This was all down to the fact he had mastered his emotions and ego. He used to say things such as "If the mind was focused enough, nothing could bother you" which I always found marvellous. I thought I'd give meditation a try as there was nothing to lose since it was good for the soul, and I was shocked at how calm I felt after. I could think clearly and felt no tension or emotions... just clarity and focus.

The next day, I felt a heightened state of self awareness and humble gratitude. Aswin also gave me a book to read about being content with the situation we're in, regardless of any level of fortune we fostered, and he certainly applied this mentality to his own life. It was an interesting read and I felt privileged to gain such knowledge. In fact, all of these conversations over the years gave me encouragement to write my own book... and here it is today.

Sitting quietly is all it takes and you can link your fingers together while crossing your feet so the energy runs in a circular motion. When meditating, either sit down or lie comfortably, close your eyes and only think of one thing at a time as a maximum. Breathe naturally and feel yourself relaxing with every breath. If thoughts enter your head, let them disappear and try to go back to a single thought.

Let your mind be clear and open, as you feel a glowing, circular energy around you. Your self-awareness and focus will heighten due to the slowdown of your environment and realignment of your senses. It really doesn't hurt to take a few minutes out of your schedule to just sit and repair your busy mind.

Keep it simple. Including this simple practice into your life will allow you to live a stress-free, day-to-day regime. If you're really stressed, meditate longer.

7

THE GREAT OUTDOORS

Being outside can really make you feel more positive about yourself and life on the whole. When you're surrounded by nature, your brain thinks differently. There is a lot we can learn from our natural surroundings; from the way things regrow after falling and their adaptation to change. Every day we face unpredictable conditions and sometimes, harsh changes. But like a plant anchored into the ground, we must learn to stay firm no matter what comes at us. We need to flourish no matter the odds, season upon season, rain or shine.

The world rotates no matter what happens on Earth. So much goes on down here on the ground and yet it still calmly does its thing, prevailing time after time. It proves to us that it is much greater than anything trying to tarnish it. Be like the Earth. Having an outdoor space you can be in really helps to clear the mind of its worries. Even if it's a small garden, balcony, or window ledge to look out from, it helps all the same. Allowing the mind time to absorb an atmosphere can realign the senses. Look out and just watch the ambience. Listen to the sounds of society in the distance and notice the elements.

Having a plant or two in your atmosphere will also help to remind you what life is all about... growth. Thinking about nature when we're caught up in drama helps us to ground ourselves. As time has passed, most of us are shadowed by high-rise developments, breathing in pollution from busy streets as we walk down the road.

We must create a balance of this dynamic in order to reach higher destinations and improved outcomes. We often fail to understand that the conditions we live in aren't actually optimised for us to create habitats in. Lack of sunlight and Vitamin D can lead to disfunction in our bodies, causing health concerns that often go overlooked. We need some light to feel positive. Gaining enough light is so important!

The outdoors is proven to boost our creativity and restore focus, leading to new ideas. Scientists also believe that inhaling airborne chemicals produced by nature can increase the level of white blood cells. And that in turn, aids us in fighting off various infections and diseases. There is so much to see and feel when outside. The trees change colours at different points of the year, weather changes in climate altering the landscape and night transforms into day. All of the answers are right there and in place to remind you we are constantly adapting and evolving.

Once you realise that our environments aren't always the best for our souls, you'll be able to start making changes that will enhance your way of living to keep the soul mentally and physically charged. After all, we mostly always have the option to do our best to improve the circumstances we are in. Putting yourself first and realising that something needs to change is what needs to be noticed.

Life can be manic, and once you're aware of that, it's easier for you to tune out from it all by embracing more of Earth's natural elements.

8

SPARK UNKNOWN SOURCES OF POSITIVITY

Have you ever been somewhere and suddenly felt a boost of inspiration appear from nowhere? These motivational bursts literally pop up out of the blue sometimes. I usually get the feeling if I visit a new part of town and see surroundings I'm not entirely familiar with. The feeling is a mixture of inspiration and wonder of what's yet to come, like a brief gaze into the future. It can happen anywhere, at any time, and all it takes is for you to be around something new or around a certain object.

Imagining ourselves in the future is good for the mind, as it helps to guide us through any rough patches we're experiencing in the present. When you look to the future, you're saying to yourself, "I'm willing to adapt to change in order to reach my potential." Instead of worrying about what the future holds, learn to embrace it. Find ways in which you can be optimistic about yourself in the coming years and picture those you'll inspire along the way. We are individual. No two of us are designed exactly the same which is what makes us greatly unique.

Strive to have mini-events lined up that you look forward to. It could be anything, like planning to visit somewhere new or trying out a new recipe when you get home. It could even be something small like cleaning the car after work or helping someone else. Whatever it might be, look forward to being able to do it. That's what a source of positivity is. It stems from looking ahead and doing things.

The thing that people often overlook is the power of the little things that have a positive impact on us. I had a car crash years ago and was devastated that my car was a write-off. But then I came to the realisation that no one was hurt, and I was still able to walk away from it unharmed. The next day, I went back to where the car was and noticed these brightly coloured plants for sale at the shop nearby, so I bought one. There was no real reason for buying it, nor did I know where it would go, but I got it anyway, simply because it brought light into my darkness. Speaking about the accident to the guy in the store made things seem more constructive, as we talked about standing back up after a negative scenario.

I went to the same shop years later, and guess what? The same guy was there and still remembered me. He said, "You're that guy that came in after the accident and got a plant to uplift your spirits!" It made me laugh and I look back on the event as a situation turned around for the better. Because my car was virtually scrapped at the time, it forced me to save harder in the hope of getting a better car. I wasn't on a huge wage and didn't know how on earth I'd regain the motivation to get back on track, but the scenario forced me to respond with courage and commitment. When we're knocked over out of the blue, we must get back up and come back with even greater resilience.

Life can be similar to a bowling ball speeding down an alley into a set of pins. The pin might be down for a while, but it gets back up every time.

9

DO MORE, THINK LESS

Sometimes beating around the bush gets us nowhere. Most of the time, it's a wise choice to just crack on with what needs to be done instead of contemplating. We are always putting things off, sometimes leaving these things until the last possible minute before we make a decision. Always tell yourself, "If it can be done now, then what on earth am I waiting for?" If it's possible to do it now, then get on with doing it.

By leaving things that can be done today until another day, we fall victim to a lazy, unproductive mindset. Be proactive in your daily endeavours and try to get the job done. You'll be pleased with yourself that you did and will be able to move forward to pastures new. When growing up, one thing that struck me about some of the local small businesses was their strong work ethic and ability to carry on.

The Patels in Brentford were always full of charisma... even when it was pouring outside. Operating day to day on an unpredictable estate towered by brutalist architecture and yet somehow so positive. Hearing that little "alright son" whenever you walked in meant you were at home. In this day and age, everyone's constantly questioning each other and putting a cloud of doubt over their heads as to why things should be put off for another day. These are the people that end up caught in a battle against themselves, forever judging as to why they should or shouldn't embrace change or overall merriment.

A classic example of this behaviour would be certain friends or family members who aren't on the same page as you. When it comes to family, the idea of deviating course can seem daunting. Very often, family members can embrace a negative mindset or hold on to grudges very easily. If we don't want to fall victim to this downhill way of thinking, we must quickly learn to be individual to ourselves. This avoids any further damage being done to our souls. The soul cannot strengthen if you do not allow it to heal.

Being slightly more isolated from drama doesn't mean you're being unfair or a traitor to the family in any way but rather, reinforces the idea that you will not tolerate negative energy in your presence. Ultimately, we can be blind when it comes to those closest to us which is understandable. However, there is no point in making so many life changes to better yourself as a human if your own house is on fire. You must extinguish the flames first in order to rebuild and renew. Don't build yourself up just to tear yourself back down again. Create solid foundations and keep moving forth without looking back every five minutes.

Learning to solidify your mentality in the thick of a disorderly state of affairs is a true test of character. Like anything though, you get used to it as you become familiar with your newly crafted vision. Being productively direct ends up becoming our second nature, sort of like drinking a glass of water, riding a bike, or turning a light on.

Happiness comes from being positive and we all deserve to be happy with the situation we're in. It's all about the energy you surround yourself in. Be the change you wish to see... it's really that simple.

Always seek the light even in the darkest atmospheres... that's how we become victorious.

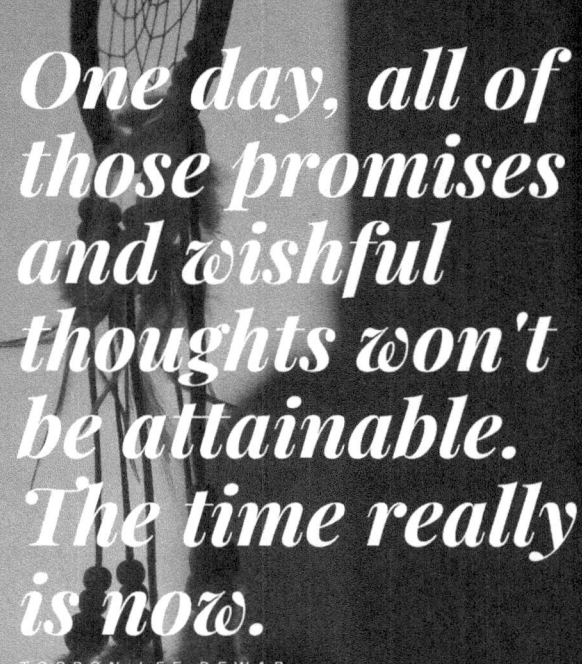

One day, all of those promises and wishful thoughts won't be attainable. The time really is now.

TORRON-LEE DEWAR

10

ANY PROGRESS IS BETTER THAN NO PROGRESS

When we've been working on something for a long period, it can be tedious, and we don't put as much effort in as we used to. Remembering why you started in the first place will always see you through. Think back to what your initial mission was and why it's important that it deserves the greatest attention.

Doing a little each day or even each week is far better than not doing anything at all. Just imagine what could've been accomplished if you threw a few pence in here and there... you'll soon have pounds. By revisiting what we're trying to achieve, even if it's a little, we are still greatly rewarded in the long run. By not trying at all, zero contribution is added to our cause and that's not what we're aiming for.

We all get busy, we all have commitments... but if we want to advance in that thing we're aiming for, we need to put some time aside to achieve the final outcome. It's easier to make excuses than to make progress. Start getting in the habit of making it easier to make progress than making excuses and anything can be achieved.

The limit to progression is what you set for yourself.

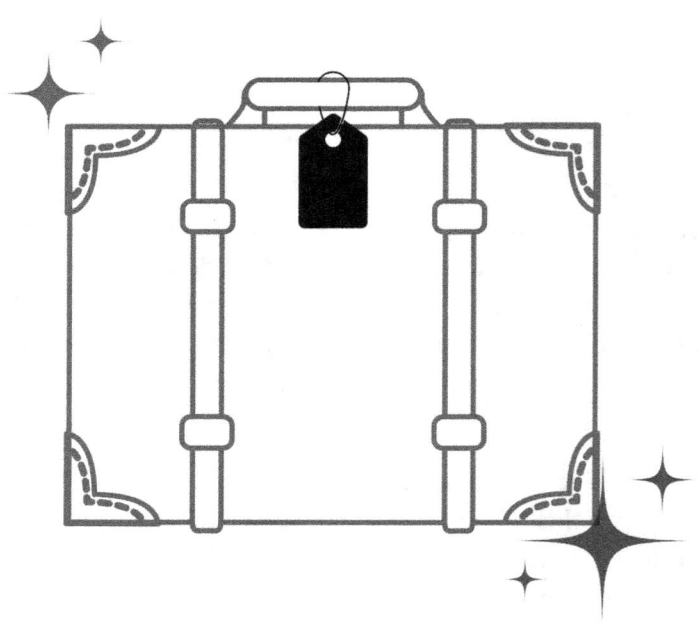

11

LEARN FROM YOUR TRAVELS

S tanding in the middle of nowhere, I saw the world from a different perspective, and it reminded me that the world is a much bigger place than we think. There was a time in particular when I travelled to Iceland to see the northern lights. Late one night, we went on a journey to the place where you could see them clearly. It was a long drive right out to the middle of nowhere and eventually, the coach stopped, everyone rose up slowly and got out.

Roaming off into the darkness to find a quiet spot, I walked around the remote area and it felt like I was on the moon. Everything around me was in complete silence, and beneath my feet was this black sandy terrain. It was actually a pleasant feeling, as I'm mostly used to crowded environments where you can see just about as far as a brick wall across the road from you. Gazing upward into the dark night, you could clearly see all of the stars glittering about. This was quite fascinating to observe, as usually, there is far too much light pollution in the city to appreciate such marvels.

Being in this tranquil zone taught me to appreciate the great world we live in and made me realise there are still places on Earth that are completely isolated. Not every part of the world is in a rush, and therefore, we shouldn't be either. Sometimes we need to disengage from the madness of today's society... we owe our minds that. Glancing around, I saw the constellations scattered about and it was the first real occasion in which I was able to spend time reflecting on how great our Earth is. After a while of searching, I saw what they call the "Big Dipper" constellation and managed to snap a picture of it. To be honest, that was one of my greatest highlights from the trip. Not buying expensive goods, not meeting famous people but just returning home with an image I had taken personally of the night stars. The simple things always bring great pleasure to us and yet we often overlook that for some peculiar reason.

I also noticed that in certain parts of the world, they do not upgrade things if they still have a purpose. Some people use less advanced tools with older-style vehicles and just maintain them well. There's a common saying that goes, "If it ain't broke, don't fix it," and that couldn't be any truer. It's all about how well you look after your possessions, not how new they are. Practicality over aesthetics is what comes to mind. Shiny new objects are always nice to have but upgrading your current objects and building upon their standard spec is also an option we can consider. It also saves us a lot of money.

Wherever we go, there will always be something to absorb... something to take home with us. As we grow up in our own domains, we can fall into a narrow way of thinking. Taking yourself out of that realm from time to time forces the brain to stay alive. Reminding yourself not to take everything in life so seriously gives you a real sense of joy. Be present more often. Feel uplifted for little to no reason more often. Life is only hectic if we allow it to be.

Whatever goes on around us will happen regardless. Whether we allow our brains to be frazzled is up to us.

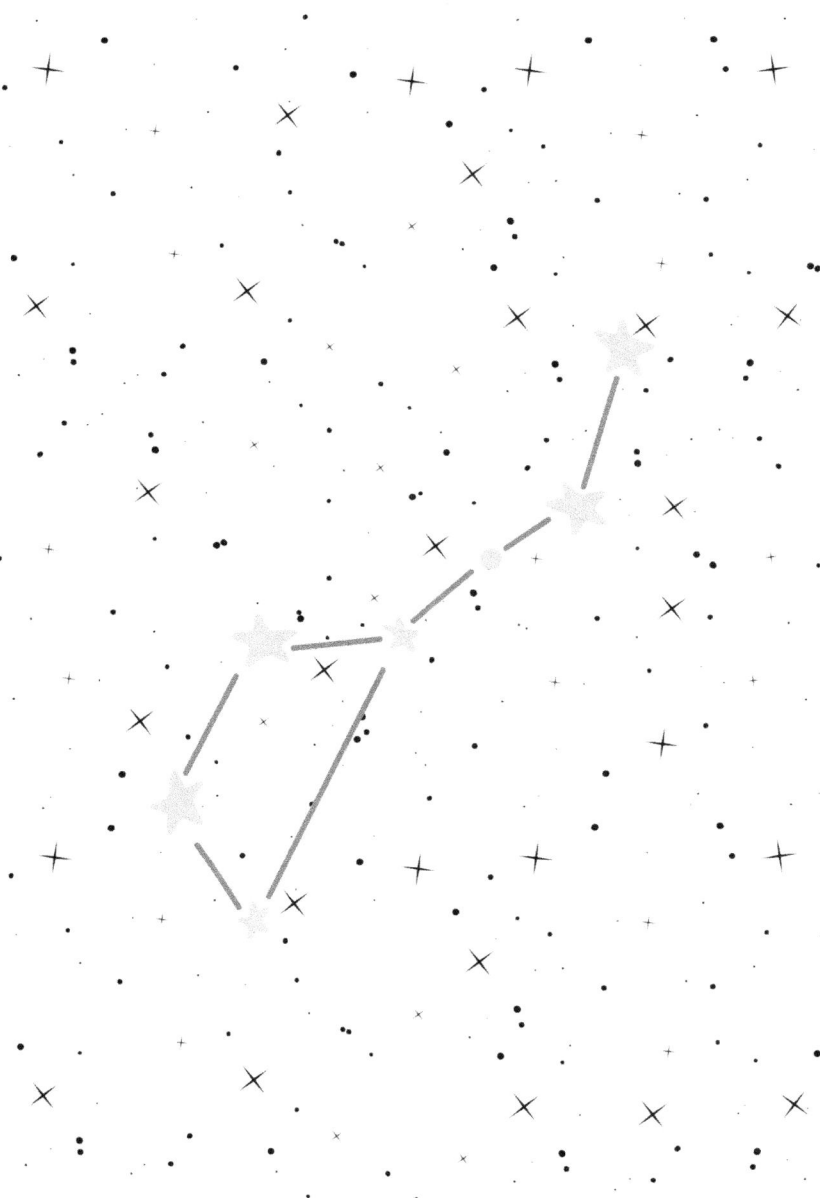

Listen

Flow

Learn

12

LISTEN MORE THAN YOU SPEAK

When we speak, we don't learn anything new. It's just a re-enactment of something we've absorbed. When we listen and observe, we are more likely to learn about new things... fresh information. If someone is offering advice, it's always a good idea to hear them out. Whether you agree or not doesn't matter because you can make that decision later. By being observant, we come across as intellectual rather than arrogant. It helps us to grow as human beings and shows that we're always willing to add to our current database of knowledge.

Sure, there are times when people's advice can come across at criticism, but that's okay. Take the useful parts of what someone said to you and learn from them. It just makes you stronger, and that's always a good thing. When we accept that we don't know everything, we're basically saying we want to better ourselves for our benefit. No one else's opinion of us matters. What matters is that you learn from it in some way if the opportunity presents itself.

We occasionally judge people and have an illusion that what they say couldn't possibly benefit us in any way. If we continue with such an attitude, we'll become dated. Allow those that want to help do just that. Everyone has something valuable to offer no matter where they're from or what they do in life. It doesn't have to be something radical that doesn't fit your ethos but rather, a new idea to embrace that'll aid you as a person. We can then proceed to grow in new ways by trying out different things we deem to be safe.

The missing piece you've been trying to find forever might be in another person's inventory. How daft would it be to presume they have nothing of interest to offer before you've even initiated in the encounter? Looking back at my own life, I've realised the most important blocks of knowledge have often come from sources you'd least expect... places others would either quickly dismiss or turn a blind eye to. When you learn to be resourceful with how you educate yourself, you gain a massive advantage over those who are simply switched off to the idea of becoming a greater version of themselves.

It's forever foolish to throw away knowledge, especially if it's right in front of you in the moment. Our own arrogance is the demon within our souls, and we mustn't feed it. We balance out any feeling of superiority by accepting that we do not know everything and the paths we explore have an abundance of mysteries yet to decipher.

We all share a common goal as humans, and that is usually to get the best for ourselves. Some people have a specially enhanced mindset which enables them to share their success with others. And when that happens, it's imperative to absorb this energy so we too can obtain richer fruits from the tree of life.

Try to listen more than you speak. The information you choose to keep is up to you.

13

IT'S GOOD TO BE DIFFERENT

Why be a duplicate when you could be a unique individual? We can achieve great things by choosing to stand out from the crowd. Going out of our way to help others and being the change we wish to see in the world is what we were made for. We don't need to copy the actions of others in our environment. Learn to use your abilities effectively and put them to good use.

For example, you might've grown up in an area filled with trouble-makers. That doesn't mean you can't go forth to inspire others. Or perhaps you grew up with "upper class" individuals and don't really mix that often. All you're doing is throwing away your freedom of discovering new and exciting areas of life. Take your life by the reins and navigate your own bespoke path. Why live from a preset persona when you could create your own? Being more open-minded allows us to make some great lifelong friends, which in turn transforms us into more versatile, educated folk. Once you understand the concepts and benefits of integration, you'll have no trouble building the best version of yourself.

Race and religion have nothing to do with failing to integrate with our surroundings. There are no excuses for not being a decent person. Avoid being brainwashed into a shattered state of mind by your fellow peers. Learn to light up paths and lead the way without seeking approval every five minutes from people who just aren't or never will be on the same page as you. Be decent, spiritually uplifted, and carve a unique identity for yourself.

I often only keep a collection of films or reading material I can either relate to or spark my curiosity into becoming a better person, and the reason for that is simple. What we keep seeing and hearing becomes a mantra, over and over again until we adapt to those practices. Why would you witness something negative repeatedly if you aren't trying to become negative? There has to be a balance... a refuel of uplifting situations that keep us sane to outweigh the deranged.

This subject can go overlooked and pretty much disregarded as something that doesn't affect one's mental wellbeing. Everything we are seeing is being taken on board, sometimes even desensitising our minds into thinking something is normal when it's really not. You might understand the contrast between lifelike and simulation, but the subconscious mind does not.

Keep polluting the subconscious mind and it won't be long before you become distorted with your way of thinking. Always reset the vision from time to time with positive viewing material. You wouldn't drive a car onto a motorway with steamed-up windows, so why continue to deprive yourself of situations that keep your brain healthy? Allow your mind recovery time from the depressive insanity that usually fogs up our clarity.

Stop living in the past of your predecessors and start living for the present. It's mind-blowing how no two people are the same and there's a reason for that. Be yourself.

Have heart in the things you do. You don't always need a second or third opinion for every last decision you make.

TORRON-LEE DEWAR

Too much thought into the process kills innovation and at times, the outcome altogether.

TORRON-LEE DEWAR

14

GOOD ALWAYS WINS OVER BAD

No matter which way we look at it, good will always triumph over evil. Having good intentions will always see you through any rocky predicaments. Sometimes it can seem as though the people that do the worst can often receive the most praise and recognition. If we think in this manner, we will become brainless. There's no need to go around acting like a clown because you're done with being decent. We all know that decent people get taken advantage of, but it's up to us to make sure we don't, whilst remaining good-spirited. If we're not careful with our careless actions when not thinking logically, we end up transforming into idiots.

Good doesn't mean weak. In fact, it's completely the opposite. Being good is being powerful and skilled enough to move through life a humble person while making sure no one abuses your integrity. Practice being pleasant but firm towards those who appear to knock your positive aura. Good always conquers the bad in the long run and it's a valuable trait to wear. Even when things don't go our way, we must stay firmly rooted in the ground. You can be distinctive... timeless. Any fool can run around acting stupid. Who would you rather be?

Our habitats and upbringings often play a major role in determining who we are. Being exposed to the same things over and over again will eventually transform you into that entity. I get how it can be a complex process when it comes to breaking the traditions of your current circle, as we fear the idea of being ousted by our fellow companions or colleagues. However, allowing narrow-minded individuals the opportunity to sculpt your life only makes you part of the problem and not the solution.

It's commonly known to be easier if we follow the flow of our surroundings, mimicking the behaviour of those around us similar to a flock of sheep. It's an excessively bland mentality that too many unfortunately adhere to in today's humanity. Many narrow minds will say that people can't help the environment they were brought up in. Which makes sense... only to an extent. We are breathing, observing, and continuously moving throughout life, which means we can, in fact, help to decide which paths to take. There is always a part of us that questions the decisions we make, and a part of us which then decides to execute that command. Saying things along the lines of "We don't have any control over the odds" is similar to saying, "I don't know what'll happen if I stand in front of that train approaching." Once we reach a certain age of overall consciousness, we tend to know right from wrong, sensible from senseless, and profit from loss.

There's no point in complaining about the world if you do absolutely nothing to change it. Ask yourself, "What impact am I having on the world... am I trying to improve it at all?" If you're not going to do it for the good of humanity, then at least do it for yourself. Be bold. Be a leader and lead by example. It won't be long before you create your own circle of powerful influencers. Others are magnetised to a strong sense of self-betterment. Don't be afraid to leave your poisonous circle of destruction behind.

Always strive to do the right thing even when it isn't a popular choice. By doing so, you become a better person.

15

DROP THE PAST, DICTATE THE FUTURE

We've all had bad experiences with people at some stage in our lives. And what we mustn't do is stereotype others based on the actions of one. Every single person walking this Earth is completely different, with their own operating system installed. It's mindless to hold a grudge against others of similar backgrounds or genders because of a daft issue you had previously. If you were to tell someone else your problems, they would most likely be on your side, so that's why it's so important to give people a chance before judging.

In the past, there were a few police officers who always stopped me at random, and after a while, it would take its toll. One day, in particular, I was mistaken for someone else and wrestled down by multiple officers for no reason at all despite my claims to not be the person they were searching for. I was tightly cuffed, my wrists were bruised, and I thought I'd fractured my wrist in the fall. I was restrained by an officer who had his knee in my back for almost 10 minutes, while the rest searched me.

When I finally stood up, my iPod was smashed, and my clothes were torn up. When I looked down, my wrists looked red and cut... you could see deep indentations everywhere. All of this happened on my sister's birthday which led to us cancelling the family meal. I was just 16 at the time and felt let down by these so-called "grown men" that had misused their entitlement of power. I heard passers-by saying things such as "Get off him, he's my teacher" to which the officers responded with swearing and unnecessary backlash to anyone trying to find out what was going on. The whole ordeal was quite a bizarre experience.

Rage swept over me and I held these officers accountable for years after the incident. I actually found it hard to move on... hard to move past this insignificant event and never had any counselling. It's only natural that we feel these emotions when something bad happens to us, but at the time, I wasn't as grounded. Eventually, I grew to accept that not all police officers carried a brutish ego and thought back to the time I was commended with an award by an officer for saving my friend's life. I only met him a few times but knew I could trust him in any scenario and that he was a good man regardless of his job title.

I knew that if he walked past that day, he would've immediately disagreed and expressed his concern for me as a human being. Mr. Diamond gave me a sense of feeling that we were the authors of our own story and always had the option to do some good in the world. Our encounter allowed me to create new chapters in life and embrace a totally new vision of who I was and what I could further become.

Back in those years, there were a lot of gangs roaming the streets, people being attacked and chased by dogs, robberies taking place, and innocents falling victim to crime. My friend happened to be one of those people. An aggressive dog was set upon him and he was frantically chased up the road. After trying to escape, he intended to open the door to a local convenience store in a rush for safety but instead, ran straight through the pane of glass and fell to the floor.

As I ran across to see what happened in the commotion, there was blood everywhere. My friend lay there covered in the deepest wounds

I'd ever seen. I knew something had to be done. The frantic shop-keeper called for help as everyone else just stood there. I knew time was running out. He was losing a tremendous amount of blood, so I pulled him up onto a chair and asked for tea towels to cover his wounds. The only problem was that he had more wounds than I could cover. But I couldn't just give up on him.

I held the wound across his head with my head whilst stemming the blood from both his arms with my arms and had my knee on his leg wound. I could see his eyes closing which made me determined to make sure he pulled through the nightmare. Paramedics eventually arrived to take over and carted him away. They managed to do a great job on his wounds, and he made a gradual recovery. The nurse later told us, without the fast actions I had that day, he might not have been alive.

Everyone spoke about the incident in school for months after, and I clearly remember walking up to the same shop and picking up a copy of the newspaper to read the story on what unfolded that day. From that moment onwards, I knew I could aspire to be more in the world and began to stand up for my own aims. I no longer had an interest in being a part of the stereotypical association we were all confined to growing up in the area.

The moral I took away from these events were that we must move forward and prove that good will ALWAYS reign supreme. Positivity wins when it's all said and done because we go on to do greater things by putting our inconveniences aside. Our lives don't go on hold just because someone else causes us grief. They continue, and if anything, continue to make us much greater versions of ourselves. These little hitches help to build who we become in later life. And if we go on to have children of our own, these experiences will help to shape them for the better through our deeper understanding of problem-solving.

When looking at the equation like this, we realise how it's actually okay to go through something difficult as we reconfigure the data into something that adds to our safeguarding.

We could all walk around using excuses about what people are like. Most of the time it's true, but don't get tangled up in an infinite battle that's a complete waste of energy. Rise above it and laugh. Winning doesn't mean taking revenge but rather, being the person no one thought you would be. And that is truly priceless. True power comes from within. Being physically strong isn't enough. You need to make your mind and heart strong enough to bear pretty much anything.

Prove to yourself that you can be more. Sometimes it's better to just save your energy for greater things. People will wonder why you're not affected by their actions, and that's the art of it all. We need to educate those around us to make better decisions on the whole. Grudges come from our pride being knocked for a limited period. Suffering is temporary. Your pride can always be restored, especially if it was out of your control in the first place. It's not about how you fall but more so, how you get up that matters.

Not allowing the past to hold us back in the present enables us to go further. We must break free from the constraints of dated ideologies that often prevent us from reaching our highest potential.

No doubting towards yourself or your worth is allowed. Just feel positive about everything and find bursts of inspiration at any given time. Your creative force must be made up of the following recipe: there is no challenge too difficult to overcome and no person great enough to stand in my way from being who I am. Once you learn to master the skill of knowing what makes you happy, you learn who you are. And once you learn who you are, no one can take that from you. It becomes etched into your soul for the world to see.

We go from most doubted to most respected with the right outlook and attitude to life.

16

POSITIVE TRANCE NO MATTER THE CIRCUMSTANCES

There will be doubters on your path, trying to knock your confidence and aims. Making yourself aware of this in the first place gives you a tremendous advantage. You'll be able to stand tall in the face of adversity, looking through challengers as if they do not exist. Being able to achieve starts with a strong mind and finishes with determination to succeed in whatever it is you're fighting for.

Be so focused on your aims that you block out all the negativity in your vicinity. Letting the evil spirits into your head only slows the process down of being victorious. The sooner you make people realise they can't come between you and your vision, the easier it will be to reach the final goal. You have just as much right as anyone else.

The reason people doubt is either because they've seen someone else fail or they've never seen what you're doing before. Once we've understood the reason for others' uncertainty towards us, we can devise a way to learn from their lack of conviction. All the answers we seek are usually right in front of us without us being aware. Keep your charismatic force of character fully charged. Having character is what separates us from the rest.

Putting your own life on hold is all fun and games until every opportunity passes you by. There will never be a right time. Just different days, some more convenient than others.

TORRON-LEE DEWAR

17

REFLECT ON A JOB WELL DONE

We forever set tasks in our daily regime, and often go from one mission to the next without any real consideration whatsoever. Stop, and appreciate how well you carried out the last job. Always reflect on the obstacles you overcame to get to where you are now and think about what you learned whilst doing so. Learn to enjoy the process as much as the final outcome.

When we get so far and are presented with a barrier, looking back proves how far we've stepped up which is a motivator to carry on. Think about all of the good deeds and work you've done whilst reminding yourself that if you've done it once, you can certainly do it again! Finding the inner strength and capacity to repeat the process will enable you to carry on going as if all the lights were green.

Contemplation of our successful endeavours enables us to move forth in a stronger motion of reassurance. Our minds positively react to us being satisfied with something we've done, so it's always good to replay those moments of victory. If we never look back on our progress, how is our subconscious mind supposed to know it's making any progress at all? Modern ways of teaching tells us to leap from one milestone to the next without any thought, and makes us feel like we are inadequate if we don't quickly line up the next goal. The truth is, a crown is made up of many components and each jewel is what makes the crown shine. Without appreciation and admiration for each constituent, the pinnacle becomes meaningless and hollow.

If you can conquer one task, you can conquer the next. Sure, there could be some setbacks along the route but that doesn't mean you can't get past them. There is no limit to progressive learning. Learn as you go along and get better with each try. If something goes terribly wrong, breathe, take some time and work out a way to get back on track. When I initially finished writing my first book, I later discovered that I couldn't export the file, so it had to be re-written. Imagine how painstaking the process would've been, especially after such a saga to complete it along with not having all the time in the world to do it again. The desire to get it finished is what gave me motivation to have another crack at it, and after a while it was recompleted. The constant visualisation of holding the finished article in my hand, and the thought of someone benefitting from a chapter is what kept me focused.

Without reflection on our great triumphs, our egos remain at war with themselves. Know that there is only so much you can do at any one time. Think of your progress like a citrus fruit. Lots of segments within one mainframe that group together to create the final result. We can often achieve so much more in terms of progress when we find ways to embrace the procedure. This makes your activities hugely satisfying and all the steps in between the start and the finish points start to feel worthwhile, and in a sense, wholesome.

Find out how it's done and what's needed in order to succeed, then go off and make it happen.

18

USE TECHNOLOGY, DON'T LET IT USE YOU

Avoid becoming overly attached to technology. If you're someone that constantly tries to stay up to date with the latest tech, you'll never win. Technology will always continue to advance and there is no end to that process. Be content with what you have and make it work for you. Technology is a tool, so use it as exactly that and not for fashion purposes. We try too hard to be the ones with the newest gear. Specifications only matter if truly required.

What we fail to understand is that cars, TVs, mobile phones, etc., will always upgrade now that there's a money-making system behind them. We're so focused on upgrading these objects consistently but fail to see we're often sold the same product in a different shell over and over again. Unless it's offering a significant benefit or having a major impact on your life, why worry about upgrading it at all?

We are blind to the fact that we are drained of our hard-earned cash for things that are usually, completely unnecessary. Money these days can be so hard to obtain and so easy to blow without any thought. We work long hours for a satisfactory amount of revenue and then spend it on overpriced cosmetic items. There isn't a lot of thought into the action of getting the best possible value for your sacred currency. Money might be everything to you, but protecting your wellbeing is always a higher priority. You'll never experience stable money if you can't even save it. Work smart, not hard, and think before you spend. Ask yourself, "Do I actually need this, and will it improve my life?" If the answer is no, then don't worry about it too much. There's absolutely no need to devote so much of your time to things that have little to no impact on your life.

We also have the opportunity to do whatever the hell we want with our finances, as we're the ones slaving away to earn it... and that is mostly true. But who really wants to live in an unbalanced ratio of unfair odds for the entirety of their life? Most of us dread the thought of putting so much energy into something and getting so little in return, and that's why it's imperative to be present. No one is preventing you from constantly rushing out to replace your current gadgets every year but later down the line, you'll be preventing yourself from experiencing other realms in life. It doesn't hurt to go easy with our spending. It teaches us discipline and sparks a greater desire to discover what we really want. We also enjoy the item more when we feel something is well deserved or necessary.

Learn how to live your life without relying heavily on technology. If there's a day where you don't really need to check your phone then don't! Leave it on the side and forget about it until it rings. After all, it's a tool for communication, not a tool for draining your time and personality away. The same goes for social media. Refrain from checking it every second and check it less frequently. Set some basic discipline for yourself, value who you are and appreciate your time on this planet. Be in the present more than the past or future.

Believe it or not, we're often able to complete the same tasks whether our tech is brand new or not. There will be the odd occasion when things need to be updated for certain reasons, however, most of the time, it's all the same.

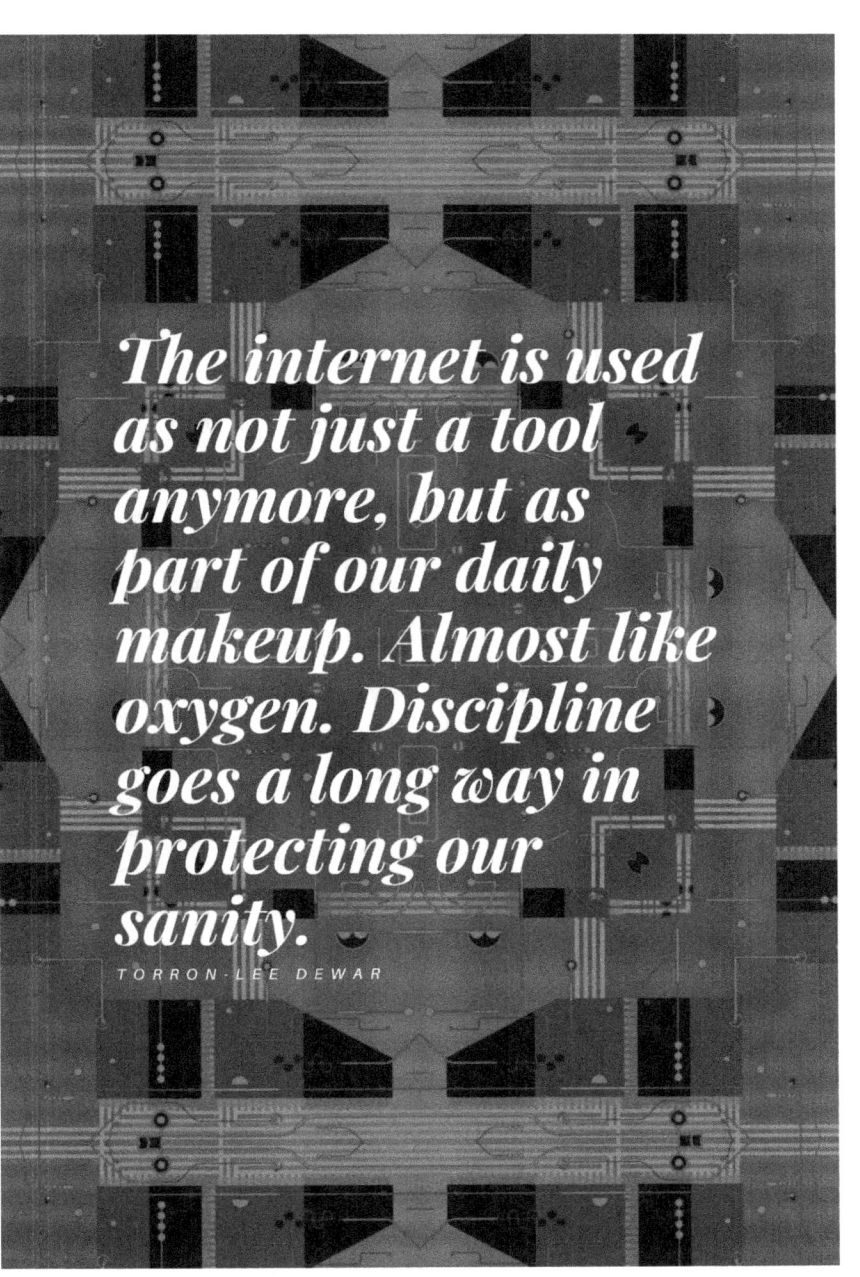

The internet is used as not just a tool anymore, but as part of our daily makeup. Almost like oxygen. Discipline goes a long way in protecting our sanity.

TORRON-LEE DEWAR

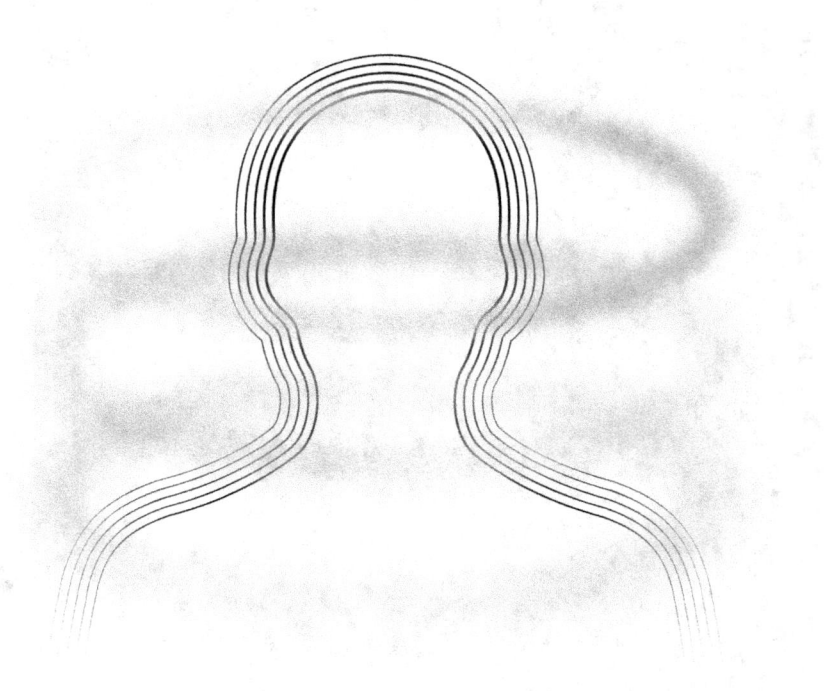

19

YOU BE YOU, LET THEM BE THEM

Being magnetised to drama isn't the way forward. Don't blame yourself for everything that happens in both your life and other people's lives. You are one person, and therefore, shouldn't try to take on the world's problems. Sure, we can always offer advice and a helping hand, which is always good. However, there's a thin line between helping and being used. We must know the difference. We must know when enough is enough before we're left sorting out the infinite aftermath of other people's affairs.

When it comes to petty situations, deflect them altogether with your newly adopted safeguarding aura mentality. There will always be drama happening in life, it's just whether or not we choose to be continuously included into the mix. The creatively uplifted have mastered the art of being selective with their time. The time we have throughout the day is invaluable and where possible, should always be spent well. Allow yourself the mental headspace from time to time and don't blame yourself for doing so.

If you think about it deeper, we need to maintain our own focus and tranquillity sometimes. If we don't, then who's going to be there to pick up the pieces for us? Be so busy living your own life that you don't have time to criticise or comment on other people's lives. Once you've offered someone the help they require from you, it's ultimately up to them what they do with it next. There's only so much we can actually do to encourage someone to change for the better. You also need to be aware that some people get a buzz out of draining your energy and will never listen to what your views are when it comes to self-help.

Have you ever been in a situation where someone usually asks for your advice but never takes it? It's even worse when that same person goes and takes the exact same advice from everyone else but never follows through when you suggest it. As humans, some of us seek out a second opinion to build clarity and reassurance on whatever it is we're about to engage in, and that's normal. What isn't normal, is that said person continuously draining the fruitful energy from you like a tap that's been left to run. It gradually becomes a waste of our productive fuel as time goes on, and if we don't reduce the surplus, we might not seek to reach out to someone who actually needs our advice.

The worst feeling is when you've tried to help someone numerous times and they fail to listen, only to take someone else's advice on the exact same subject. When that happens, it's best not to waste even more energy by taking it personal. Just understand that some people won't relate to you but might relate to others for whatever reason. Just don't keep using your limited supply of energy on the individual if they've already got it covered.

It's tempting to hop onto what someone else is doing because it seems like a fast track to success. Do you remember erasing your own work to copy someone else's, only to find out they were wrong anyway? That's what can happen quite often in life.

Be decent, focus on improving yourself, and above all, find ways to self-motivate!

66

20

LIFE. POLITICS AND RELIGION

Life isn't about being number 1 all the time but rather, enjoying every moment for pleasure instead of recognition or benefit. Everyone's so caught up in politics, religious affairs, and general drama, that they forget how to actually live and fulfil their own lives. Being caught in a net isn't exactly living your destiny.

Ever wonder why you can't just be you? Why does life always have to be about following someone else's trends, demands and beliefs? We don't have enough leaders in the world. People spend most of their lives worrying about things that either don't exist or don't concern them. We must be open-minded if we want to learn about the earth we walk on. Copying the ill actions of another can lead to bad decisions because we end up falling into a brainwashed state of mind that we no longer have control of. Brainwashed people end up believing that anything is justifiable because someone else said it is, and don't even stop to consider what's happening in the present.

As humans, we are capable of doing so much more if we keep our vision clear whilst staying humble without the belief that something or someone is more superior to another. The problem with society is people try to live via dated protocols... striving to apply these procedures to the modern world. People fail to realise that society evolves. So in order for life to make sense, those beliefs must evolve too. The issue with things like religion, in particular, is that most of the time, our ideologies do not evolve and thus remain stagnant in time. As humans, we like to be in denial, and cease to accept the possibility of becoming more openly adaptable to living a life of freer nature.

It's not to say that there's anything wrong with believing in something specific... it's actually good to believe in something that gives you motivation in life. We all have our own little system that keeps us on the rails. It only goes wrong when we do not evolve and apply realism in today's society. The first step to self-improvement is desiring to be better. We can either choose to ignore the fact that the world upgrades each day and be limited to what the mind can conceive or, we can embrace leadership and be more open to new things that transform our characters beliefs into a vital framework, which benefits us far greater.

Learn to respect one another regardless of religion, and the world becomes a very warm place. In one of my workplaces, I had a multitude of colleagues who each fostered their own identity. We would all sit around a table whilst waiting for the shift to start and talk about how we thought the day would pan out, as well as what we were currently focusing on. If anyone looked over at the table, they would never assume there were many different beliefs among us. And that is the point. Religion should never divide us. The strongest team is often also the most diverse. It's also perfectly fine to evolve your beliefs as time advances. Evolution is natural and healthy. Religion without sense is like a car with no wheels. You can be in it, but it won't take you anywhere. We must be logical and good-natured if we want it to take us places for the greater good.

Closed-minded souls can only travel so far before they hit a barrier. The greatest achievers adapt to change, and that's why they influence so many others around them.

21

WHAT'S HAPPENING NOW IS
TEMPORARY

Each new day comes with different mysteries. No matter how far ahead we plan, sometimes surprises can still pop up out of the blue. Being adaptable to change is only the first step of overcoming life's barriers. When we're dropped in situations we do not like, we must remember that we still have the opportunity to come out on top.

In a 24hr day, each hour is individual. That's 24 blocks that are yours to do with as you wish. When we are presented with a negative moment, we often let it ruin the rest of the day... and sometimes the rest of the week. If we let it ruin our week, we've lost 168 blocks of what could've been positive, productive time spent. Sometimes it's easier said than done, but why let someone or something steal all of your other life blocks when they've already taken one from you?

We always tell ourselves we're not going to stress about the petty things, but it happens to the best of us. One thing that annoys me is when I feel like I'm being taken advantage of, especially when I've been polite. For example, there was a time when I had a minor problem with my car's speedometer, so I went to a local garage to find out what the problem was. The guy said I should leave the car with him and he would call me when he found out what the problem was. He also made out that he'd only charge for labour i.e. 1 hour at most but would call me regardless before doing any work so I could discuss further.

A few hours down the line, he called me up demanding I had to pay an extortionate amount for the job despite no parts needing to be replaced. When I turned up to the garage, I was reluctant to pay the full amount, so he dropped it by a mere few pounds. I was in a rush and didn't have time to argue, paying the money with a clenched fist. The initial agreement we spoke of was clearly abused when he failed to call me to give an idea of what the problem was and what would be involved. I always like to diffuse confrontation, but sometimes, the need for strong reasoning is completely necessary.

I was so annoyed with myself for paying for what I could've done myself at home. However, sometimes we can't always see fate coming until it's too close for comfort. To make matters worse, the mechanic had somehow smeared a load of dog mess into my car's interior floor which although comedic, only infuriated me even more at the time. All of these things are pretty insignificant when you think about it, but when we're in the heat of the moment, things are always seen from a different perspective. It's the principle behind people's actions that concern us.

There was another occasion when I needed to help my mum find a car because her previous one had become unusable over the years. I searched for days until I came across an advert online for what seemed like a decent, cheaply priced vehicle. I went to see it, checked it over and everything seemed okay, so I bought it, took it back, and spent all day cleaning it up and topping up the fluids. I later drove it to my mum on her birthday and she was pleased to have her wheels back once again. Before I had purchased the car, I went for a test drive and the man explained that everything was in good mechanical order and that there were no problems whatsoever. Just over 24 hours later, the car completely cut out on the road and the engine management light illuminated on the dashboard. My mum had the family in the car and had to wait hours for recovery to attend. When I found out about this, I was just mortified because not only did I feel a strong sense of accomplishment having found a working car but also, the man sat opposite me with the greatest confidence stating how nothing would go wrong. I tried to call him and there was no answer, so I messaged him, and he told me there was nothing he could do because it was "sold as seen." He didn't care one bit about his advert saying no mechanical issues and told me to go to trading standards if I had a problem with him selling vehicles. I later discovered that he was a local conman in the area swindling thousands from hard-working individuals... so I wasn't the only one.

The thing that got to me the most was how that money was now lost, as the car couldn't possibly be resold and had to be scrapped. The car had a hidden plethora of problems which were masked, and this rendered it unroadworthy. I knew it would take a while to finally make the money again and that my family were back to square one in being without transport. The notion of innocent people being taken full advantage of is a very hard pill to swallow, especially when you're a person with high morals.

We can only learn from these dull situations we end up in and remember that it's not the end of the world. Sometimes it's the small things that get to us the most and leave us with a feeling of aggravation. Go home, have a tea or whatever you do to relax and laugh it off. It's always better to try and find humour in negativity as opposed to continuing the rage. Know when to let go as well. Refrain from chasing something too much. Once the issue has been somewhat sorted, let it go and move on to new things no matter how mad you are feeling. Knowing when to move on can restore internal harmony.

Anger causes stress, and stress leads to health problems. Just try not to make the same mistake twice in future by doing a little research.

Those with the greatest minds do not live within the limitations of man-made stereotypes.

TORRON-LEE DEWAR

22

SEE THE BIGGER PICTURE

F orget our differences. Anyone with an assumption that one of us is somehow inferior because of the way we look is purely uneducated. Those who segregate others only segregate themselves and stop learning the day they choose to become narrow-minded. No matter what size or shade of the spectrum we are, it will not determine how much we can advance mentally and physically. We do that naturally by choosing to better ourselves.

We don't just belong to a single race but rather, a human race, and it's vital to remember that. We are all born into the world as a blank canvas. What we see is absorbed into our operating system and shapes us into our character. This is why it's essential to gain the right energy and surround ourselves amongst those who see the world openly and equally. There's no other way to get ahead in the world other than maintaining balance, and most importantly, being positive. Too much of our daily energy gets drained on the topic of how we look and where we're from. If all of this energy was diverted into a more meaningful manifestation, we would be even more advanced as a species than we are today.

We must understand that race, social classes, flags, and so on were created to divide and establish personal insignia to those who wanted to advance in their own endeavours. The funny thing is, we still live in the shell of this matrix that has somehow been set for us many moons ago. If someone randomly approached you and demanded you follow something, you'd most likely be skeptical. So how is it, ideologies that were created before we were born are so strongly followed and embraced when we know nothing about the reasoning or origins of the idea? Strange isn't it? It's the fear instilled into the common follower with the idea that leaving the regime results in being judged. Most of the time, people will follow and praise a concept for their entire life, not realising they've only lived a fraction due to their dated, restrictive beliefs.

If we weren't meant to be different, then everyone would look entirely the same, but as you know, that isn't the case on Earth which encompasses a variation of skin tones. It makes sense why there are so many variations of people when you think about it. The concept of individuals originating from different climates and terrains, creating an adaptation of what our body needed at the time for that specific environment. It's strange and exceedingly unethical when someone tries to downplay another person based on how they look or where they're from.

Only a certain number of the world's population have unique minds. These are the people standing on the outside looking in... the ones who don't follow the masses. It's far more rewarding in all areas of life to be a custom-built individual rather than part of a batch production.

The one that's different often has the odds stacked against them but usually ends up with the biggest rewards, so it's always worth it.

23

WE ARE WHO WE ARE SO BE UNIQUE

There is absolutely no sense in wishing you were someone else. We were all created for a purpose. Once you discover your life's true purpose, you'll only want to be yourself.

Sometimes we don't really know what our purpose is, and that's okay. Doing positive things you enjoy, like helping others, expressing your artistry, or developing things, all count towards the person you are. We often think we need to be in one field to truly know who we are, but the greatest minds are in many fields at once. Unlimited mindsets go further than a one-track mind, purely because of their versatility and ability to morph.

Don't even attempt to fit in with society... there's no reason to. When you go outside and take a look around, everyone's driving the same vehicles, visiting the same stores, and wearing the same if not similar outfits. Anyone can do that. Why would you want to mooch through your valuable time on Earth desperately trying to blend in? Are you a brick being cemented into a formation or a gemstone that grabs curiosity?

I was at an awards evening in Birmingham and noticed that the majority of people were dressed in such bland footwear, and I was the only one with shiny black shoes. I suddenly thought, "Have I worn the wrong shoes out today?" but came to realise that it wasn't me with the problem... it was everyone else trying to fit in with what is considered the norm. A lady in the lift complemented how nice they looked. Would I have got the same response had I wore something that made me fit in? I doubt it, and that's the point. We feel positive by being different, and those around us will be inspired by our actions and wonder how they too can be different amongst the crowd. Find uniqueness in your own endeavours and don't be afraid to enforce it.

It's the same concept when you visit someone else's house, and they have some unique furniture or flooring. We comment on how nice it is and then it inspires us to save up and perhaps, buy something just as nice in the future. The snowball effect of unusuality is not to be underestimated.

Overall, it's how we apply these ideas to our everyday cycle that counts. You don't have to roll out in a palm tree shirt to be divergent. Just be yourself and enjoy being yourself in a positive way. Those who don't try to fit with the norm are often the most successful and happiest beings.

Forcing yourself into the mold uses even more energy as opposed to just doing your own thing. So you can see how this mentality could be destructive and counter-intuitive over time. Without character, the world wouldn't be great. So for the sake of mankind not being so gloomy, have some character.

We probably waste more energy worrying about what others think of us than we do actually living. It might not seem like a big deal, but in the end, it really is.

24

PUT ENERGY INTO THOSE WHO ACTUALLY INTERACT

All too often our life energies are readily available for others to drain. If someone doesn't make an effort to engage with you after you endeavour to communicate then it's time to ditch the connection. Our time is worth more than a repeated deflection of our energy, so it must be used in the right places if we're to feel uplifted in return. If you feel like you're always carrying an excess load of burden, simply take the rucksack off.

When it comes to helping others, we must help ourselves first in order to help others in the first place. What use are we to others if we haven't met the requirements of our basic needs in advance?

If you feel that you are being deliberately avoided for long periods of time, the energy isn't flowing in both directions. For relationships to be healthy, the direction of enthusiasm must travel both from and toward us... think of a circle. Each New Year, it's always good to reflect upon how energised people made us feel in the previous year. A decision must then be made on who we're going to keep with us in the New Year and who we're not, it's as simple as that. Everything that operates effectively has a two-way transfer of energy when you consider it.

25

UNCONTROLLABLE CREATIVITY

Today, we are expected to fall in line. Copy each other, and not to diverge onto unexplored paths. Society is angered at those who show an interest in seeing life from new angles.

Without knowing it, we are unawarely forced, as if brainwashed into a nocturnal state of mind.

If we take a look into times passed in ancient history, their craftsmanship and methods often seem far more advanced than what we have in today's age. Sometimes it seems as if we've gone back instead of forward in certain aspects of creativity. That's because people weren't afraid to let their creative curiosity run free. We're expected to keep quiet and sit behind a screen on a day-to-day basis. It's no wonder why our imaginative mindsets have dulled over time.

We watch TV, slowly disregarding the need for our own selves to be creative. We think that no more can be done to improve who we are and the world we live in. We think that society doesn't need our innovative input, as it sees enough from others... surely?

Well, that is wrong. We allow mankind's ignorance to trample on our artistic aura, which is never a positive thing. The reason we are often told that something can't be achieved is because many others have tried and failed in that specific topic. What people don't see is that sooner or later, someone will come up with the solution to the problem. We must dare to be different if we're to evolve. If we don't evolve, we remain still in time. No one ever stood out by being the same and blending in with the crowd. Creativity is the key that opens the door to success on many occasions.

Don't fear the criticism from those that claim success can't be achieved. Strive to prove them wrong by finding a way to make it work for you. Pessimists often blurt out statements such as, "No one's ever painted a fence blue, so I don't think it's a good idea." Or "It's completely unacceptable to use such outlandish experimentation when it's never been heard of before."

The problem with dismissive people is that they shoot down the construction stage of the process before they've seen the outcome. It's really odd because everything must pass the construction stage... nothing just happens. Always bear that in the back of your head when dealing with these demons. That is all they are, demons hiding in human makeup.

Instead of being so eager to conform to standard, we should first ask ourselves why. The others chose to copy the norm, but you don't have to when it comes down to personal expression. Have you ever noticed that no one cuts their garden lawn in ages but when one person decides to, many surrounding neighbours choose to do the same? Why do you think that is? A coincidence? No. Inspiration to improve? Yes.

Thinking about the creatively, analytical mind, there isn't a lot of information as to how structures like the pyramids were built. There's speculation from many theories, but one thing's for sure... they didn't have the machinery we have today. If humans discovered a way to haul lime-stone blocks over 130 metres high to create a structure more accurate than some of today's buildings, then what's stopping you from achieving what you want out of life? Each block weighed around 2.5 tonnes, which is like lifting a car. Think about how we would struggle to carry something of such weight so high on an inclined sloping structure. The point being, most of the things that terrify us in modern life aren't usually real issues, so why hold back when most of the time, we have the resources or ability to achieve more? We are often privileged to be in the position we're in, more so than those asked to haul limestone blocks in the raging sun.

Once you understand that you probably have more than most, you begin to exercise your power more effectively with confidence. Sometimes you have to witness or feel something to awaken your inner drive. Compassion mixed with determination yields insane results.

When I visited these structures and regions in person, I felt an unexplainable surge of motivation. I remember returning home and thinking no obstacle is too great and no challenge is too big after what I had witnessed. Going inside the pyramids was even more intriguing because of the network of tunnels leading to secluded rooms, which felt absolutely still, as if made to last against the test of time. The precision and conviction towards the concept of these structures and artworks was hard for the mind to comprehend due to our ever-taught limited way of thinking about things.

Don't limit yourself to life's boundaries... it'll hold you back. You either make excuses for the circumstances or you take charge and make the odds favour your desire to emerge victorious. Stand up for positive impact, the world needs more of that... much more. Let your great ideas be heard. Become the person you want to be, as there's only one opportunity to do that.

Don't wait around because time waits for no one. We are far more resourceful as humans if we step up. So start today.

26

STAND UP TO THE DEMONS

L et's face it. Life has its setbacks. Some are more predictable than others, but there's no telling when drama will strike next. Do you ever wonder how you got yourself dragged into a certain situation despite coming so far in life? It happens to the best of us, and usually at the worst of times. Life has its demons. It's how we fight them off that matters whilst we walk the path of our daily regimes.

Difficult people that enter your life shouldn't be allowed to make you feel inferior. When you feel yourself slipping into a fiery conversation, stand your ground in a calm and collective manner. Take a moment to think about what the person is saying before responding. Sometimes, people are so used to dominating others that they forget who they are, or who they're talking to. Let it go over your head... your time is just as precious as anyone else's. Just let the person think they have the upper hand, but don't be afraid to state the facts on why you think they're being unfair or unreasonable.

It's good to ask the person if they can justify their claims, and elaborate on why they think their statements are fair. Sometimes, they won't even know the answer to this type of question... responding with unrelated jargon in their defence. If you want the upper hand in a conversation you feel isn't fair, state concrete facts calmly with confidence and it won't be long before the debate flows in your favour, as facts don't lie. Some debates however, never end and your energy shouldn't be used up too much trying to prove a point.

When you stand up to bullies and aggressive people that are used to getting their own way, change happens. Sure, they won't like the fact that you're challenging them, but if the world is to be a positive place, we must be the change we wish to see. Don't wait for someone else to do it. Being bold motivates the crowd, and we're stronger in numbers, so don't be afraid about what extent your abilities can reach. For example, someone might disapprove of a project or idea you're working on. It won't make your life easier by agreeing with the person knocking you down... only harder in the long run.

People in the workplace are often passive-aggressive. They will ask you a question and when you answer it they will try and make you feel stupid for no reason at all. Some people are just like that and don't need a motive to be overly aggressive towards you. That doesn't mean you need to tolerate this behaviour though.

When we let narrow minds knock our confidence, we lose. Not just in that moment, but for years to come, as we grow to accept the concept of allowing others to kill our creativity without much effort into questioning why. If you really want people to listen to you, speak up on what you think matters. Be who you are. We inspire those around us to become better versions of themselves if we first, believe in ourselves. Once we have faith, anything is achievable.

When you wake up in the morning, just know that you have a purpose for your existence.

People need your positivity, and when they feel more positive, it makes you feel more positive. It's the circle of energy that sparks inspiration.

27

CLEAR ENVIRONMENT, CLEAR MIND

I t's no word of a lie that having a clean surrounding can make you feel much more positive throughout the day. Whether it's your living space, workspace, or transport space, being in a clean surrounding is always a plus sign. It might seem like an insignificant benefit to our lives, but it's actually one of the most important.

When the space around us is accessible and clear, we are able to get to things much easier, which goes in our favour no matter where we are. Tidying up throughout the day will ensure your spaces are clutter-free, and you'll be happy each day because it won't build up and overwhelm you. Before you leave your home, do your best to clear things away and reset the layout of everything. It doesn't have to be 100% tidy, but just focus on the walkways being clear, the carpet vacuumed and the work surfaces clean. That way, when you return later that day, it'll feel like you're walking into a showroom which is always a great feeling inside.

The same goes for being organised. Sorting out things such as accounts, car maintenance, and bills in advance will save us and prevent last-minute stress. Sometimes it's not always possible to get things done, and that's okay. But what isn't okay, is making excuses, and putting things off until the next day when they can be conquered today. When we learn to make productive use of our time, it comes naturally and becomes a default thing for us to do. Once you've managed to find enjoyment in solving issues, it suddenly doesn't feel like stress anymore. We are made to believe that certain things are unpleasant or mundane but that can be changed around by altering how you see the task.

It's way better to learn to enjoy the so-called boring things in life rather than sit there trying to pull through it with a bad attitude. Anything can be altered or made to be more enjoyable. Experiment here and there so you can start figuring out ways to make tedious tasks pleasant to engage in. Tasks can usually always be made more enjoyable whether it be upgrading a monotonous spreadsheet that needs some colour added in, or a car ride you don't enjoy that just needs some good music for the journey.

Write down all the things that you either find terribly boring or usually avoid, and then write ways in which you can add better buzz to each situation. Once the list is complete, start altering each task by putting it straight into effect. Get into the habit of turning your fate around the moment it starts to become draggy. Waiting so long for a miracle to happen just worsens the pain of it all! Making amendments doesn't usually take long and has far greater benefits to our mental health in the long run. So stop making excuses to put your enjoyment on hold and start now!

It's a hell of a lot easier to be creative if all of your tools are clearly set out in front of you... ready to take on the task.

28

USE TIME, DON'T LET IT USE YOU

Time is one of those things lurking in the ambience. Constantly ticking over in the background whether we like it or not. There is absolutely no need to persistently check the time throughout the day unless you have to. If there's somewhere you need to be, or you're trying to beat a record, then that's a good use of time. If you're monitoring when the best time for you to sleep is, or you check the time to calculate things, that's also a good use of time.

When checking the clock in our spare time for no reason, that's basically living life in a cage. Why look at the time if you don't need to be somewhere? We find ourselves doing just that as a force of habit, but it's not clear why. Over the years, we've grown so accustomed to looking at a clock, as it's so accessible to us.

Time appears in the corner of our computers, on the menus of our TVs, on our phones when we pick them up, in our vehicles... it's everywhere. But just because it's everywhere, it doesn't mean we have to check it if we really don't need to. The continuous burden of time can worry us throughout the day and can even prevent us from enjoying ourselves during our own free time. It either helps or hassles us. It's always wise to learn the difference between the two.

29

FIND ENJOYMENT IN PROBLEM-SOLVING

N o scenario can defeat us when we learn to find hope or enjoyment in finding the solution. Discovering ways to enjoy problem-solving rather than stressing often helps us to find the answers much quicker.

Sometimes, we come across people that aren't even trying to hear what we're saying. For instance, people in "authority" with a condescending attitude might be something you have to put up with on a regular basis. The most important thing to remember is that nobody has a greater level of self-worth than you do. When we remind ourselves of this, our issues become much easier to resolve because we gain confidence to query the things we do not agree with.

Without your consent, it's impossible for anyone to make you feel subordinate, no matter who they are. Being reserved makes it easier to overcome the ordeal with clarity. This is something you'll be able to improve upon again and again until eventually, setbacks and negative energy won't bother you.

We must refrain from allowing anger to control our emotions. The calmer we are, the more control we have to gain positive outcomes.

Not everything can be solved with the knowledge of modern humans. Some scenarios call for a completely unknown way of thinking.

TORRON-LEE DEWAR

30

COPING WITH LIFE'S DEMANDS
AND WORK

During a time when I was juggling many issues at once, I'd have intense dreams which reflected what I was experiencing in the real world. One, in particular, was fighting many people at once. When I looked into what it could mean, I was surprised to find out that it resembled the lengths I was striving to go in order to achieve change. It meant that I was putting in 100% day in, day out to the cause relentlessly.

It can be tiring to constantly max out day after day. Sometimes, it may seem like we're fighting a constant battle that simply cannot be won. Don't beat yourself up about it. Carry on and reward yourself from time to time while reminding yourself why you work so hard. Praise your endeavours, and soon you'll know why you put all the effort in at that very moment in your life.

It's challenging to see the finish line when we're surrounded by the fog of uncertainty and never-ending setbacks. At times, it can feel as if we've circled the world twice, only to be greeted with a blow to the chest after all of our many endeavours to do the right thing. This is all part of life, and all we can do is turn the lights of positivity on full beam. It's a matter of time before we end up exactly where we want to be... it just takes a hell of a lot of patience and determination.

There should always be a balance. In the work environment, I often saw individuals punching the clock day in, day out, which caused them to burn out in the end and become depressed. Endless overtime, a lack of direction and overall passive-aggressiveness all being common traits in the corporate industry. Extreme lifestyles shouldn't be matched with extreme periods of isolation but rather, a plan should be devised to create stability, health equilibrium, and overall ability to accomplish the task in the first place. If you find the perfect balance between rest and work, you'll never feel like you're at an extreme end of the spectrum.

The idea is not to feel overworked and not to feel lazy or unproductive. We're always happier when we find some type of enjoyment in our work and the body functions better when our needs are met. Because we need a healthy body to complete work tasks, our health should always take precedence. Listen to what your body tells you because without good health, you can forget the wealth.

Some people often feel the need to do things outside of their means and run on empty until they bite the dust. Nothing can run on an empty power source as it must be generated from somewhere. Learning to enjoy your job or finding work that enables you to feel good makes it that much easier to enjoy your time on this earth. Regardless of what anyone thinks, everything needs balance. Find more reasons to feel great and embrace vibrational happiness, even when there's no reason.

It's vital to learn when it's time to fight and when it's time to fall back into chill mode. Looking after our own needs first makes sure we're able to move forth.

31

RUFFLE A FEW FEATHERS

I f we are going to excel in our field and be awesome, we must be prepared to ruffle a few feathers in the process. This doesn't mean one should act in an aggressive manner to achieve their goals but rather, by upholding a polite and precise outlook. Don't be afraid to speak your mind a little when the going gets tough. In today's world, we try excessively hard to entertain those in power and don't like to be the ones that upset or disgruntle someone that isn't giving us what we want. When a situation isn't going our way, it requires a spark of fulfilment to make the opposition aware that you're not a pushover.

Looking back, I recall a time when I needed the permission of a senior executive to advance our charity's plans of opening a new arts centre. Without his help, it would be a right old challenge to see the job reach completion. The first time I spoke to this man on the phone, he was abrupt, condescending, and generally disrespectful. His ego seemed so high that the conversation we had didn't even make sense after a while. By the time I came off the phone, I was irritated and went out to clear my head. I kept wondering how I would overcome certain barriers if he wasn't going to be on board. A few months later, I attended an awards evening and happened to be seated right next to him. He didn't know who I was, as he had never seen me in the flesh before and only knew me by name. He maintained an enormous smile on his face projected at every one at our table, displaying his nonchalant banter as he engaged in peculiar conversations. The time had come, and he turned across to me, asking who I was, so I slid him a business card across the table. He looked down at the card and back up at me with a kind of, perplexed motion and said, "So you're the guy everyone's talking about?" with a somewhat surprised look on his face, bearing a half-grin.

I didn't say too much, but he went on to interrogate me about my plans to improve the community. But before I could finish, he started to apply pressure and turn up the heat. Questions began to fly at the speed of light to the point where answering them would just be silly, so I stopped engaging in the conversation. Deep down, I could feel myself becoming slightly heated as I defended my stance, but you know what they say. Arguing with an idiot makes you one as well, so I wasn't about to plummet to that sort of level.

The night went on and I barely gave the bloke any attention. What seemed to confuse him further was how everyone else on our table seemed to engage in great conversation toward me, speaking favourably of my former work in the area. This added validity to me as a person, and that decreased his limelight. Sometimes, saying less is more powerful than trying to prove you're the bigger person. There will be occasions where you don't need to communicate verbally in order to reveal who the bigger person actually is regardless of age or background and so on. Situations like these taught me a lot about myself and the unhinged society we live in.

Some people will always take their power to the next level by trying to look down on the rest of us as mere insignificant beings. Too often, we're afraid that we might upset someone if we challenge their abhorrent behaviour. The thing is, we can sometimes cause more damage to the rest of our agenda by not speaking up when the time is right. Feathers need to be ruffled in order to advance.

Don't agree on everything at the blink of an eye. Think about it first and then challenge it if need be. Those who are successful always strive to even the odds to benefit them and not just the opposition. Arrogance is not to be confused with polite confidence in your own endeavours. It's perfectly acceptable to stand up for what you believe in, especially if it's a positive thing. Standing up for your aims shows that you care and are willing to do something about the existing issues posed upon you.

If we always worry about what the next person thinks, how would we get anywhere? How would we ever make any progress? Taking a while to notice that we must step outside the comfort zone in order to reach the next level will help you to understand when it's time to ruffle a few feathers. Never feel guilty for desiring to improve yourself and wanting to do the right thing. It's better to overcome a little self-progression guilt than to live the rest of your life with unfathomable regrets.

When the habit of doing what you believe in is greatly enforced, a sense of self-pride is felt... and the snowball continues to roll, building itself more significantly with each motion. You'll begin to realise that so much time is wasted in contemplation, and that's never a good thing. The world is huge and it's going to challenge you. There are well over 7 billion people roaming the Earth and there's no telling who we're going to come across next. But who cares? Be positive and confident regardless because there will always be someone who doesn't approve of us.

People will judge you for doing pretty much anything, so do you... and do it well!

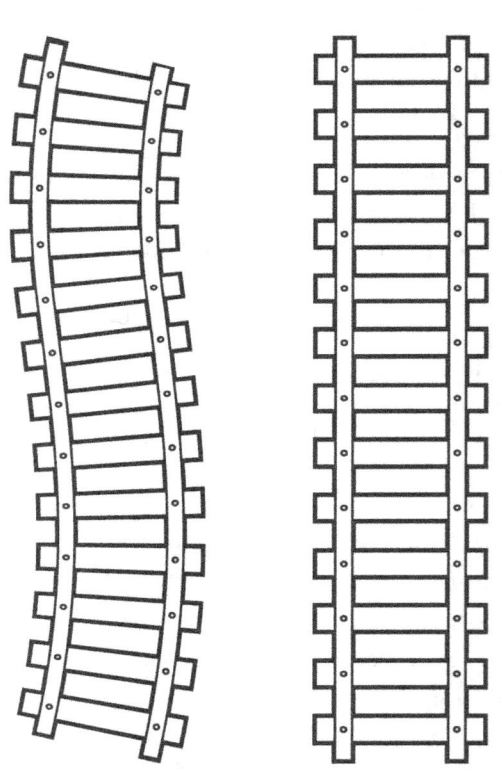

32

EXPRESS TRAIN TO SUCCESS

Making it perfectly clear what path we're on shows the crowd we aren't messing around, and plan to move forward by any means. It's important to present yourself in a way that makes it crystal clear to people that they're either on your train, or watching it blow past at 100 miles an hour.

It's not selfish at all to be committed to our desires. In life, acquaintances either keep you chugging at a steady pace, or they try to slow you down. Obstacles must be ploughed through like they never existed in the first place. Being halted by negativity thrown onto our path simply isn't an option. They say we become just like the people we spend most of our time around, which is true unless we've identified the characteristics of who we surround ourselves with. It's good to remind yourself of this mantra from time to time: "I know what I'm aiming for, so I won't become brainwashed whilst in the company of so and so."

As long as you know what you want in the future, it doesn't matter who's around you, and this shouldn't be an excuse for becoming dull. It does, however, help to have more inspiring and positive minds in your vicinity to keep you on track, as their outlooks will eventually rub off onto you in some form. It's alarming how quickly someone else's negative emotions can transfer over to us, and we need to be aware of that in the back of our minds. Review all of the things that are happening in your life at the current moment, and pinpoint what is winding you up, getting you down or just generally giving you a deflated vibe. It's easier to lead a more vibrant month if you know exactly where the root causes of your unhappiness lay.

Some people say if you're the best one in the room you should find another room, which is true to an extent. At times, the room with the least toxic ego is the room where you can get on with your aims without feeling the strain to compete, thus taking your eyes off the prize. Again, it all goes back to having a balance of both motivation and a productive environment. Yin and yang. Coming to terms with what balance really is and how it can help you on a daily basis is crucial knowledge.

Getting a little bit of this and a little bit of that makes sure we're operating in a well-rounded fashion. It also helps to control our own egos and stimulates the mind in good capacities because we're exposed to different frequencies. The person with the most experience or understanding of multiple elements usually goes the farthest.

A plant withers away around too much darkness yet flowers to its best potential around a sunnier environment. You're no different when it comes to the energy you allow yourself to be watered with.

33

THE CIRCLE OF GIVING

Doing the right thing makes us feel great. We do the right thing because it comes back around in ways that are often unexpected. It's not about getting things in return.

Bringing out the best in others and contributing to their wellbeing and quality of life motivates us to grow as strong-minded people. There's a certain little buzz that radiates within us when we witness how our actions played a part in improving someone's life. And at times, we won't fully understand that feeling until we're caught in the crossways. By getting on with things without thinking about getting anything in return, we entice a flow of good flowing energy to enter our environment.

When we help others, we help ourselves in many areas of our own lives. It's quite a subconscious thing we do without fully realising. More than often, we reach out to others because we imagine what it would feel like to be in that position. We sympathise with whatever is going on in front of us and want to be of use, especially in a time of chaos. When you do something good for someone else, you feel great about it for a long period afterward. Giving back makes us feel like we have a purpose in life, and that's the kind of buzz we need to keep us mentally healthy. One must experience the feeling of that transfer of energy which doesn't just travel one way. Once the intention leaves your body to do good, it rebounds in a similar fashion that light does to a mirror.

Our good deeds come back around to reward us, and the positivity just keeps on spreading. Always bear in mind the importance of being humble. A little help goes a long way. There is something called "The Butterfly Effect" which encompasses the belief that little, insignificant events can later lead to significant outcomes in time. For example, you chose not to help someone struggling with their shopping, and because of that, they fell and injured themselves. As a result of that, they couldn't go to work the next day, which resulted in your train being delayed which meant you missed an interview for a dream job. This is just one of many variable outcomes that this concept harnesses. Sometimes it even affects us in ways that aren't directly connected to us but impacts something or someone else somewhere along the line.

You might think this is quite an extreme example and how the consequences could surely never touch us in such a capacity. The funny thing is, reality is more than often a lot closer to home than we anticipate. The thought behind this notion isn't to try and do everything by the book but rather, to increase your awareness of how something we say or do can have substantial consequences as we go on. We think because the world is huge, there is no point trying to fix anything at all because it won't benefit us. But the harsh reality is, as humans, we're a little more connected than you think... especially in the smaller communities that make up our towns and cities.

And really... the bottom line is, we should always be keeping a level head. It also goes both ways as well, so ultimately, reflecting back to yin and yang. Not too much of one thing or another but finding that harmonic balance as we navigate through our journey. Have a think about where the imbalances arise in your own personal life and what you could do to restore the overall balance. Are you overworking and not dedicating enough time for yourself or your family? Are you mentally disconnected from being in the present due to living in the past or too far into the future? Are you not exposing yourself to new, stimulating things each week? What we do now determines what happens later. It might be minutes away, hours away, days, or even years away. Who knows.

You never know. The person you just helped might bump into someone you know and end up helping them later down the line. They are more positively charged to help because of the energy you gave them earlier on.

34

IT'S NEVER THAT SERIOUS

Refrain from stressing over things that simply cannot be changed. There might be rowdy neighbours that keep you awake till all hours, and the council isn't taking your complaints seriously. Or, you don't see eye to eye with a certain family member but have to see them every week. Instead of getting worked up about these inconveniences, accept that it won't change so you can find a way to work around it.

When we accept that we cannot change something, we give ourselves peace. Peace in finding new ways to alleviate our problems. Always try to discover the most stress-free solution to every setback. It could be something simple like wearing earplugs or having your TV on a low volume (set on a timer) to create a nicer ambience to help you sleep or finding ways to spend less time around pessimistic people who drain your soul.

I'd always battle with the idea of feeling as though I've let the offender win if I wore earplugs or avoided situations I was meant to be present at. It wasn't long before I realised it wasn't them who was winning... it was me. It's aggravating at times when we feel like we've let our guard down but it's always best to refrain from wanting to teach people a lesson. We can't let other people's nonsense take up our mind's capacity. Our mental state is worth more to us intact as opposed to polluting it with the chaos of strangers. Save your brain-power for the more rewarding endeavours when it comes to little grievances in day-to-day living.

Perhaps something on the lines of drinking chamomile/herbal tea and having a warm bath before bed to help you unwind are some of the things that could help. I found that using an essential oil diffuser helped to create a pleasant ambience in the evening, whilst switching my mobile phone to the "do not disturb" mode at a certain time made sure I wasn't being harassed by stressful calls when it was time to switch off. The last thing anyone needs is to receive a call at 9pm with someone on the other end demanding something from you. Protect your sense of peace and don't apologise for it. It'll not only build respect towards yourself but also from others as they begin to under-stand your boundaries.

Downbeat situations can always be adapted to if not avoided alto-gether if you want to increase and maintain your feeling of overall positive sanity. Usually, there's always an opportunity to avoid bad encounters, so take it. Try to always select the path of pleasance before it gets to the intervention stage. Watching a hilarious film whenever you feel irritable will most certainly restore your mood. Life is always so serious, but it doesn't have to be because we are the authors of our own stories.

Blank everything out when you feel life getting tough. Focus on yourself, do something pleasant and the rest will fall into place eventually.

35

BE STRONG AND GOOD-NATURED

Don't hold onto anger. It imprisons you. As a teenager, I'd become so angry to the point where I wouldn't be in control of my actions. I came to realise that this worked against me rather than in my favour. The rage within has to be controlled if you're to emerge from the scenario with the upper hand. Nowadays, something could wind me up and I'd have forgotten about it less than 10 minutes later (most of the time). The old me would've held a grudge for days, if not weeks after the incident took place, which wasn't a good thing.

Learning to forget about conflict and moving on keeps you mentally stable, and it's the right thing to do. You really don't have time to constantly bear the burden of negativity on your shoulders. It wears the soul down after a while.

You don't need to have the last word either. That's a fool's game you're better off not playing. Remember, that clutching onto anger can impact your health terribly. The more tension you let go of, the better you're taking care of your mental health. Only you can do this, no one else, and it's good to be aware of. Anger only demonstrates that you're not in control of your actions, which is never a good thing because you become vulnerable.

It's okay to feel a little annoyed at times... it's a natural instinct if someone has done something bad to us. But holding onto that anger isn't okay. It's far better to learn from the issue than to direct any more energy towards it. Brush off the annoyances and move the hell on with the greater things in life.

Very few people have mastered the art of being good-natured but resilient at the same time. People are either considered too soft and get taken advantage of, or so busy being defensive that they become isolated and pessimistic. We mustn't be too much of one or the other... the medium is what we should be aiming for.

When someone lets us down or causes upset, it can interfere with our pleasant side because defences go up. They shoot up so high so no one else can repeat the same actions on us. This, in turn, can push good people away that might actually benefit our lives in the long run. On the other hand, if we're too freely open, others can see this as a weakness of being readily available 24/7... mostly for the wrong reasons.

Tune out from general madness and adopt calmness. Embracing the cool and collective trait beats being manically mad all the time. Problems that get flung in your face should be handled in a smooth, appreciative manner. You might not agree with these issues posed upon you, but that doesn't mean you have to show hostility towards it.

Learning to be in between will make sure you get the best out of life and don't miss any opportunities to improve your innovative mindset.

Being humble and good-natured whilst standing up for yourself and being resilient in tough times is what builds a creatively strong character.

36

THE ART OF SELF-RESPECT

Respecting ourselves is one of the highest priorities on the list. Without self-respect, it's difficult to move forward in the world to make a real impact. If we want people's attention, most of the time we need to prove that we're worthy of it. Having respect for one's self means that we've acknowledged our own basic needs and this, in turn, gives off an appealing vibe that will draw people to you. When practiced regularly, it's not something we must think about repeatedly. It'll just happen subconsciously. It'll become part of the aura that makes us who we are... part of the mainframe.

No one has the right to make you feel less important, and when you stand up for yourself, you tell the world, "I'm confident about my purpose in life and what I'm striving to achieve." This kind of aura draws opportunities towards you as a charismatic person. It's always good to believe in yourself, even when no one else does. If anything, it should motivate you more when people don't see your worth because we then push harder to prove them wrong.

I'm personally motivated when someone doesn't take me seriously, and I'll do everything within my power to switch that perception around just to see their reaction in the future. Of course, we don't need to sink to someone else's level to entertain their perception of us, but it's a brilliant psychological training exercise when we learn to repel narrow minds. It's a priceless feeling to rise above and beyond people's expectations automatically and effortlessly. Whilst we strive for healthy successes, our souls quietly build in the background, thus evolving into robust, creative forces with an enhancement of upgrades. Don't get tangled up in emotions when it comes to respecting yourself. It's not a hard process to master and will benefit you and others around you when it comes to negotiation, incidents, and other situations that might unfold in everyday life. You are you. And you have to protect you.

Feeling nervous energy is an emotion that takes a while to extinguish. When you realise that you're a human, and the person who makes you nervous is also a human, then what's there to be nervous about? They've got something to offer but so do you. They've got skills but guess what... so do you! The playing field can always be levelled. We can always upgrade ourselves in one way or another to be more supreme. Self-respect doesn't mean embracing an overinflated ego... it's much different to that. Think of it as a likeness to a tree. The tree doesn't ask for permission to grow, it just grows and does its thing whilst providing oxygen to the atmosphere. It knows that it has a purpose, so it carries on, and there isn't much else to it. Take on a tree mentality, doing what you need to do, leaving a trail of good behind you. You don't need the permission of pessimists when you're trying to do some good in the world.

In the end, your good traits will be magnified because you had the courage to step up. Pushing yourself to do something that challenges a disapproving person can be scary at the best of times. We get a rigid feeling from within, and sometimes even feel sick when thinking about taking someone on. Sometimes, causing a temporary upset is necessary if it means we get a brighter future. After all, if you're trying to do the right thing, then who gives a damn and why do we over-think it so much? Negative minds will get over it sooner or later, as they find someone else to target. And by then, you'll be well ahead entering a new chapter on your thrilling quest to improve.

Over time, it'll just become second nature… sort of like riding a bike. Your character will level up in ways that might surprise you.

If you aren't being treated in a decent manner, speak up. Sometimes you have to fight the storm of pessimism to reach the sunny island of contentment.

TORRON-LEE DEWAR

37

MAKE IT YOUR MISSION TO STAND OUT

I t's not good to follow trends. Why? Because trends come and go just like the sun in England. Setting an example for yourself eliminates the countdown to irrelevancy, as you're creating a style or persona that is unique from the rest. You're sculpting yourself into something you see fit... not what someone else sees fit.

Every day we're concerned about what others think and how they see us. The only thing that matters is how you see yourself, and how you imagine yourself becoming the person you want to be in a few years from now. If concerned about what people think, why not give them something to worry about? Keep working on yourself and those very people will fear that they aren't doing enough in their own lives.

When we embrace individuality, the world stands to attention and says to itself, are we doing it wrong? This is the ultimate point. Don't fear that you're doing it wrong, let the others worry they're not doing it right. If everyone lived by this mantra, the world we know today would be vastly different in all aspects of creativity, design and procedures which benefit our lives.

Unfortunately, a lot of the time humans waste far too much energy replicating the people around them. So much, I've witnessed others desperately trying so hard to follow the same fashion and sports interests as their peers, drinking heavily and being outlandish just to prove their masculinity somehow. There's nothing less masculine than someone who follows suite just to try and blend in with people who don't really care about you anyway.

Thinking back to Aswin earlier on, he came to the UK in 1975 from India but was born in Kenya, which I had no idea about until he passed away. This reflects how there is always so much to learn about people, even when in regular contact. His shop was one of the last to don a fairground style carousel horse outside that glittered in the sun. You'd push 20p in, hear the coin drop and then the machine would suddenly activate, catching whoever was on it off guard which was part of the thrill. When the other shops stopped selling penny sweets, he continued to. The shop also sported a photocopier down one of the aisles and this is what made his shop stand out compared to the others nearby.

Being bold is not about brash power, masculinity or promoting an authoritative position but rather, about endorsing the idea of becoming an upstanding member of society. Just imagine if all the energy individuals threw away towards mindless endeavours was used to find ways to improve ones own self. We would be immensely surprised. Having an electrifying creative aura is one of the highest possible skills you can have. Knowing how to harness your own inner power to expand the mind is one of the greatest underrated talents you could possibly own. Invest in building yourself and you can never lose.

The first step to standing out is to believe in yourself and your own practices.

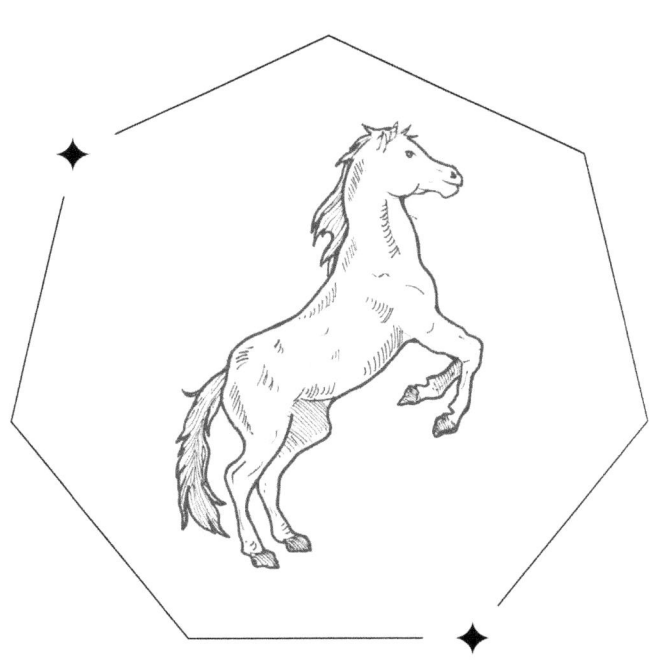

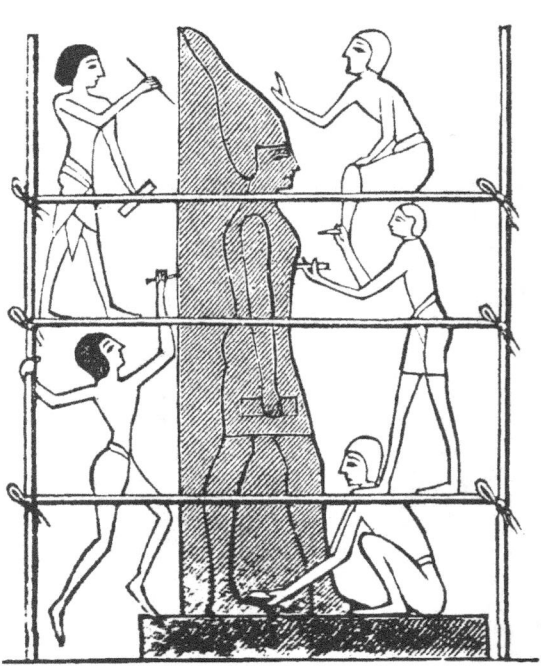

38

THE CREATIVE DON'T HAVE
COMPETITION

A common mistake we make when it comes to goals, business ventures and dreams is the belief that there is a competition. The belief that somewhere, someone else has either already done it or is more capable of doing it. Sure, we acknowledge the fact that there may be others of a similar nature to us but they're not our competition. They are similar... never the same. It's crucial to understand the difference, and equally important to know that you can't be overtaken if you're putting your all into something.

Most people spend more time worrying about their "competition" rather than the improvement and consistency of their own endeavours. This is what creates a taxing downfall and puts the others ahead of us. When you invest so much time into what you're doing, there can't possibly be a competition that offers the exact same experience. Nothing is ever like for like down to the last strand of motion. Latching onto and exploring the mentality behind this reasoning will enable you to go where most can't. It's deeply relevant in all endeavours of life, especially when it's business-related.

If all you worry about is competition, your ethos and values will fade away. You'll become a competition head and end up having nothing real to offer due to being so caught up in other people's productivity. It's okay to take a glimpse into someone else world but it's forbidden to spend unhealthy portions of time there. Keep working on your vision and give it more attention than the ideology of rivalry. As time goes by, you'll be glad you spent more of your energy working on yourself as opposed to seeing what the next person is doing every five minutes.

This goes for everything in life including relationships too. When you keep looking for more to the point of extreme scrutiny and picking up on every little thing, it makes it extremely difficult to just be in harmonic peace. This is also why screen time on the internet needs to be sensibly managed. Having so much access to a never ending supply of information just makes things worse, as you never feel fulfilled. Too much of your time is spent dabbling in other peoples affairs etc.

Just stay on your side of the fence more often. Learn to get on with living your life in the greatest possible way, as there simply isn't enough time to follow other people's progress whilst making sure your own is attended to. You're either pouring productive fuel into your own tank or throwing shed loads into someone else's economy without even realising it. Stop leaving your house of wonders unattended because that is a sure-fire way to burn it to the ground unintentionally. Make it your mission to stand out, pride yourself on your own uniqueness and the rest takes care of itself.

Theoretically speaking, if you spend enough time pruning your own garden, the flowers of success will bloom colourfully without a doubt. There's no need to keep checking every second if someone else's garden is better. Just stick to your own and don't keep leaving it unattended!

39

THE TIME IS NOW

Everyone waits for the right moment. Don't be everyone. If you feel it's the right moment to act and you've done your research, then go for it. As the saying goes, "Time waits for no man."

The sooner action is taken to improve your life, the better. There's a thought in our minds that tells us it's better to wait. It's what we've always been told throughout the years of growing up. Waiting never got anyone anywhere. It's good to be patient but not so good if we do not act at all. People think that not acting at all is being patient but it's really not. They are in no shape or form the same thing.

Patience means the subject is still in your best interests whilst you're waiting for it to happen... following up on its progress every now and then without getting too flustered. Meaning, you're still very much aware that what you're waiting for is still in motion. Not acting at all means we think the plan is in motion when really we haven't the faintest idea what's happening and aren't doing anything about it!

It's quite easy to fall into the trap of a lazy mindset. "I'll do it tomorrow" or "I'll do it when the weather is nice" are just common excuses for not getting on with it. If the opportunity arises to get something done and it's safe to do so... get on and do it! You'll feel pleased you did, and this might even lead to a surge in the mind's productivity.

If an opportunity to succeed presents itself, take it... especially if that opportunity presents itself on more than one occasion. You'll soon find out how it's done if you're unsure, and that is often the best way of improving upon our current knowledge. It's often better to try something and drop out later if you don't enjoy it than to not try it whatsoever. How are we supposed to know without being involved?

How many green lights do you need in order to proceed?

40

DON'T LIMIT YOURSELF

I t's extremely easy for us to create limitations that prevent us from going further to accomplish the unknown. Growing up in an urban environment, I felt that life had its limitations and no-go zones. The belief that one could only be a success if you hit straight A's in a test and went to university was what held me back. The fear and pressure of not being up to par with everyone else would tarnish my own aspirations I had for the future. When we're young, we have all of these great aspirations for the future. And then suddenly, we hit a certain age and all of those dreams are somehow snatched from us.

In our minds, we think it's daft to aim too high, and rarely bother to even give any thought that our ideas are worthy of anything. When you stick to your character regardless of whatever someone's saying or doing, you'll achieve great things. Only those who dare to be different make an impact. Always remember that.

The fire inside me to do well is what took me on an adventure not many had been on before. Sculpting a brand new path and leading the way for others that didn't fit into a particular category was what followed from embracing a unique mindset. Trial and error is what most always fear. Stepping out of the comfort zone is imperative in order to experience things that are commonly unheard of, or unseen. It feels almost alien to throw yourself into something that not many follow because there is no path to follow... no lights to guide the way... no plans to see what errors lay ahead. General worry must be eliminated by giving yourself a chance to move forward and experience an improved lifestyle.

Life isn't a one size fits all scenario and yet somehow, we're made to believe it is. When it comes to advancement of opportunity, try everything before dismissing it as unworthy of your time. The only way to discover who we are is to experiment with how situations and environments make us feel. If never faced with the unknown, how would we ever find our calling in life?

What works for that other person might not necessarily work for us. Get out in the field and find out what works for you.

*We humans, believe
we know it all.
When you think
about the vastness
of the universe, you
begin to realise we
know nothing other
than the limitations
of our own
environment.*

TORRON-LEE DEWAR

41

EVERYONE ELSE DOES, DOESN'T MEAN YOU HAVE TO

The majority of society blends in. but that doesn't mean you have to.

Peers in school or at the club like a particular sport but that doesn't mean you have to.

Society wears similar mundane dress codes but that doesn't mean you have to.

People in the area where you live carry negative attitudes but that doesn't mean you have to.

Workplace colleagues keep quiet about suggestions that improve their lives but that doesn't mean you have to.

People give up easily after being told it's not possible but that doesn't mean you have to.

Everyone follows the same linear path in life because it's what's expected but that doesn't mean you have to.

When we think outside the box and cut off the strings that control our lives, we open up endless possibilities and an array of options to visualise the character we could become. Everyone's always telling you how to act, what to wear, what to do. Why don't you decide for yourself for a change and set an example? Striving to follow my own ideologies for example, resulted in being able to carry the Olympic torch. Now in any ordinary world where one follows the norm, that would not have been possible due to the lack of innovation typically found in a mundane circle. Once I had discovered the uplifting sensation of setting trends amongst my own circle, it really didn't make sense to revert back to "normality."

It was a mind blowing day, and I remember it being extremely hot outside... literally sweltering heat. Thousands lined the streets, and the general ambience was actually surreal. I hadn't seen this many people look so happy all at once. As we travelled along the route, I could hear people cheering... celebrating... radiating positive energy. It was all just blurry background noise as the heat from the lit flame was blowing near my face... and strangely, that felt good. It was in that moment I felt what living actually meant... being in the present.

There will be times throughout your life when you are so immersed in the moment, it's almost as if you've elevated off the Earth's surface for a few moments as you experience something majorly moving. And even when others don't or can't relate to your high, it doesn't impact the experience you feel any less. This was one of many events which happened that switched a light on inside my head. And when it starts to burn bright, you suddenly realise how much time you've wasted trying to fit in to something substandard. Setting your own standard is always a winning choice. You don't need to fit into a certain group or category when you've got your own aura.

It's refreshing when we as humans, learn to embrace who we are as individuals. Get on with experimenting, learning, and raising the bar. Just don't be in a manic rush to fit in.

You're not a puppet, so why allow society to pull the strings throughout your entire life?

42

LET THEM HAVE THEIR LAUGH NOW

We all get those days when we feel like people aren't taking us seriously enough. People are mysterious, and sometimes it's never clear why someone treats us differently to the crowd. Often, we find ourselves thinking, what does it take to get a little respect out here in this day and age as we struggle to understand the bizarre attitudes of those around us.

Although irritating at times, our heads must be held high so we can continue along the path to success regardless of who's giving what level of respect we desire at the time. It won't matter down the line anyway because when you're aiming for something, you've already worked out what you want.

Someone's ignorance toward your desires of victory is irrelevant. All you need to do is focus on what you're doing... focus on what's making you happy right here in the present, and it won't be long until the foul attitudes of mankind are quickly turned around.

When people fail to take you seriously, keep working until they have no choice but to take you seriously.

43

FORGET THE PREMADE STEREOTYPE

Clear the stereotypical image others premade for you and just concentrate on doing well in whatever makes you excited in life.

There have been countless occasions where people in higher positions have spoken down to me... purely because of who they think I might be and where they think I might come from. They think, "That guy" is a typical person not capable of having the knowledge in order to succeed. What they don't know is how "That guy" has tried and failed numerous times to get where he is today, who has devoted most of his time trying to improve the lives of those around him in the process.

People will doubt your abilities, and you shouldn't let it get to you or prevent you from doing well in the world. Let your achievements and successes do all the talking. Judgemental, condescending characters have rarely made a positive influence in society, so what does it matter?

When you look at the behaviour of animals, they don't suddenly stop doing something because they realise they're a different shade of fur.

Those barriers just aren't there for them. So ask yourself, why are they such a problem in our world? The truth is, it all depends on how you see yourself. How you project your own self speaks volumes to those around you. It's a great feeling to be judged and then to be taken seriously shortly after. What makes our journey rewarding, is the overall struggle we face in order to reach our goals.

Most of the time you will notice people being ignorant. Living constrained lifestyles, believing something is right just because a person looks similar to them. This is a backward mentality that often holds back raw progression.

There were times in the past when I'd believe that someone might be on my side with something in particular due to the fact of them having a similar background and image. Only to find out, I was totally wrong, and that the person had ulterior motives, which ultimately didn't include helping me at all.

The strange thing about modern-day life is how we're expected to be like and trust the people that look similar to us. Almost as if we're being magnetised to a specific colony and hit with a bogus ideology that we'll be safe so long as we stay within the perimeter. It's actually the worst thing we could do, as there are good and bad souls hidden within the cosmetic appearance of what we call race, religion, and gender. These are just categories someone made and somehow, we just fell into them as we grew up.

In the process of this modern upbringing, we are tricked into false concepts and scared into not thinking freely for ourselves. Following blind advice that usually harnesses ulterior motives is one of the worst things we could ever do.

When you think about living your entire life within a category someone else made for you generations back, the idea of stereotyping yourself becomes less and less appealing. You'll start to do whatever you can to no longer remain in this confined, limited, zoned out perception of life we start our journey in. Step out of the cage and into the paradise.

If we enjoy the obstacle course set out for us, no challenge is too great.

44

THERE IS NO LIMIT TO LEARNING

School can teach you about general topics, a textbook can demonstrate how it should be done, but that should never be the limit to teaching yourself how things actually work in the flesh. Ring-fenced learning can only take us so far and give us an idea of what the world is like. To truly know, we have to see what's out there and adapt ourselves in the real world.

Some things cannot be taught in a school. Knowledge must be absorbed by real situations that take place in everyday life. The standard template can only take you so far before you're categorised and expected to make a decision as to who you want to be. The only way of knowing who you want to be is by experimenting with different hands-on work; travelling and engaging with people and experiences you're not familiar with.

I always had an interest in martial arts, and one day, decided to take up classes in Wing Chun which helped to increase my confidence and overall movement. The instructor, Roy Fretwell was such an encouraging person I could instantly relate to and I ended up learning so much from him. Wing Chun taught me about breathing techniques, power from within, and self-discipline. There was so much more to it than what met the eye... so many benefits that could be applied to the outside world. The energy transferred from Roy's personality and artistry was highly motivating. That energy could then be taken and deployed in other areas of my life.

Getting out there and taking in the sights, the scents, and the ambience is what makes something click in our minds. Being present in the midst of energy is something real, and until we've been near it or experienced it, it's always hard to judge.

We can be told how to ride a bike and even look at the diagram in a textbook on the procedure. We could also watch a video of someone else riding a bike and even hear sounds on the mechanical operation of the bike. But until we've actually ridden the bike, we will never truly know what it feels like. What's it like to ride the bike downhill at speed while it's raining in poor visibility? What else is the bike capable of whilst in motion?

I guess we only find out once we try it for real. Don't assume that everything has already been learnt. Your experiences are just the tip of the iceberg and there is no limit to self-knowledge.

Keep upgrading; you don't need to only be in a place of tuition to actually learn new things. Valuable education spouts up everywhere so acknowledge and absorb it.

45

RETREAT, RECOVER, REVISE, RETURN, REPEAT

Overworking without rest is sure to work against us no matter what anyone says. Never allow someone to call you lazy just because you know how to look after your mental health. After grinding on a plan for a period of time, take a break to renew your mind. Sometimes we aim, keep missing our targets and never think to question the bow itself. We have to switch up the approach and methods we use in order to hit the target right in the centre. Thinking time needs to be allocated so we can begin to create a master plan.

Going away to think about something is what enables us to climb up to the next step. It's challenging to reach a higher level without thinking about how you're going to get up there. A train doesn't move without its tracks underneath and a car doesn't move without its wheels. And even when it does have wheels, it might go further up the road but needs a steering mechanism to guide itself further... beyond the main path and into a brick wall. This is why others' negative opinions on what we're doing aren't relevant.

When you can't move forward, devise a plan on alternative ways of making it past that barrier. Prevention should make us work harder.

People walk away from a locked door because they can't find the right key. There's always another way to overcome a barrier and that just involves crafting the correct key so we can access it. Creativity is the magic that allows us access into uncharted territories.

When posed with an obstacle, no panic or intimidation should be dwelled upon. Locked doors are why keys were invented.

Even if you take longer to work out how it's done, that's surely better than walking away altogether.

46

STAND UP FOR A CAUSE AND BE
HEARD

I f you were once in a position where you weren't heard or listened to, chances are someone else is too. There will always be others experiencing similar issues as you are, and it feels good to set an example. Giving people hope that they too can emerge on the other side of the water makes us good leaders... strong pillars in society.

When we back ideas that were shunned in the past and motivate others facing the same struggles, life is easier to understand. We learn things about ourselves and discover who we are when choosing to fight for something. Giving back has infinite future gains in many aspects. And at times, the rewards aren't even clear until much further on. We have to clutch the idea of planting seeds now so we can harvest the rich fruits of our labour as the days advance.

When life has a purpose, it's easier to get things done... easier to understand the path we're currently on. Devoting ourselves to a particular cause or project can yield fantastic results, as most of our energy is invested in that area and not spread mindlessly across the field. Like a juice, too diluted and it tastes weak, not diluted enough and it's totally undrinkable. It's all about finding that harmonic balance and learning how to perfect the final outcome, which sees the results you were looking for.

You deserve to be heard as much as the next person. When you comprehend and follow that ideology, you get the most juice for your money. Meaning, you get the best of what life has to offer because you manifest your own reality. Getting excited about something and then following through with it raises mighty self-esteem within us.

If you can't reinforce and stand up for something in life, are you really living?

47

PROVING THE DOUBTERS WRONG IS A GREAT FEELING

I remember when I was trying hard to get into college in the final weeks of leaving school. The teacher writing my final grades on the college papers assumed that all of my results were low and wrote D on a subject without even looking at what it should be. I then watched on as he made a weird face and had to cross it out to replace it with an A.

I said nothing and felt good inside at the same time. Instead of taking things personally, we must see the funny side in people's arrogance. It sets them back in their own lives. The feeling of being doubted and proving people wrong becomes addictive and should be used as raw motivation to progress successfully.

Turning negative attitudes into positive ones is a good trait to have because it boosts your productivity at the same time. So really, the jokes on the one doing the doubting because all they're doing is making you more determined. Arrogant people stopped learning a long time ago because they believe they're higher than everyone else and that's their downfall.

We all learn in different ways and you should never doubt yourself because of trivial things like what mark you scored on a test paper. Some of us don't do so well, some of us do... and some of us a bit of both. It all depends on your definition of "doing well." When it comes to learning, do what works for you and forget what people scream in your ear. What works for them might not work for us, and it's important to grasp that. No one is perfect... that's what makes life so diverse. If we were all the same, life would be utterly predictable. Sooner or later we would all be bored out of our minds living in a forced, artificial society.

It's not down to anyone else to decide how successful you are. I've met individuals who others wouldn't consider being intellects, yet when you have a conversation with them, you become fantastically open-minded and inspired. We all have something to offer and you're the only one that can discover what that something is. Use those gifts for the greater good. Intellect without positive intent is like a blossom tree surrounded by bricks.

So there you have it. Just because a person appears to be smarter than you doesn't necessarily mean they're going places.

Do your best where possible and you can never fail.

48

ABSORBING THE WORLD

Travelling opens up our minds to new possibilities and teaches us about things we've never seen before. When stepping foot in a new city or environment, we realise how big the world really is and how much there is to explore beyond our typical setting. There is so much more to life than following the same regime, experiences waiting to be felt... food waiting to be tasted, and so on.

In the months around writing this book, I was privileged to travel to Switzerland to lead an interactive show with a team of artists from the UK. I didn't really know what to expect and the tour threw me in the deep end, teaching me how to adapt to changes in order to meet targets. Early mornings and long days made me feel exhausted at first. But it wasn't long before I grew accustomed to what I needed to do and in the end, I felt better than I was the week before. When I returned, I felt stronger, more inspired, and pleased to be a part of it all. New experiences are daunting, to begin with but once the motion gets going, there really is nothing to fear.

Not only did I go somewhere I've never been before, but I also made friends with other artists that came from different walks of life. In that short space of time, I felt like I had made some great new friends with interesting stories to tell.

New experiences push us to learn and achieve more. Sometimes you never really know what you like until you've tried it. We surprise ourselves when we're introduced to what we're not familiar with. I came back feeling motivated with a taste for green tea due to drinking it every morning before starting the workshops. Like anything in life, if you keep doing a little of something every day, it won't be long until you're doing it all the time.

Not settling for a basic job was always my aim, and even if Switzerland were the only place I'd travel to for years to come, it would still feel like I found my purpose. Your life might consist of a mixture of things; it doesn't have to be one thing like the generic life handbook says.

Travelling motivated me to experience things more. Next on the list was Greece and then Portugal... each adventure sparking new ideas of what I'd like to be doing in life. Seeing new landscapes can open our minds to bettering ourselves and can push us in the right direction when our current daily lives become bland. New experiences always thrust us further in life, and sometimes, we surprise ourselves with what we can do.

Whilst in Greece, I hired a car, and it was a left-hand drive. I had only been confident to drive right-hand drive but gave it a go anyway. It wasn't long before I was cruising around the country in a drop-top Jeep with complete confidence.

Later that week, the opportunity arose to visit an island not far from where I was staying. However, to reach it, I would have to drive the boat there myself across some pretty deep water. I was nervous about doing it purely because I'd never done anything like that before. After learning the controls and basic procedure, I gave it a shot. At first, like anything, it was daunting to think about, but the fear was soon overcome halfway across the water. When you accomplish one goal, it sets you up for the next goal like a chain reaction. Sometimes you have to just get on with the task at hand and learn as you go along.

> Travelling is never a waste of money, simply
> because of all the benefits it gives back.
> Sometimes it's hard to say why it improves our
> lives, but once you've travelled to a few places,
> you'll know why.

49

BOOSTING PRODUCTIVITY IN
THOSE AROUND YOU

Those closest to us will learn from our actions, so it's always important to set the right example and show them the correct path to take. Life is made easier for us when we do this, as those around you will be on a similar page and we all go on to learn from each other. Energy rebounds and isn't to be underestimated.

When family and friends learn to utilise positive energy, everything flows. If they're having a rough day, bring them back up. When you're having an off day, they will bring you back up. The time you invest in your everyday environment will reward you and everyone else in the vicinity. Not helping someone that has fallen over on the way to work would paint you as someone with low morals. And of course, sooner or later, that would bounce back into your face when it's least expected. And the reason for that is down to not being in the present.

Everyday living is no different, so aspire to boost the confidence and positive outlook in those around you. If people are experiencing a dark situation, give them light. Being a beacon of hope to others not only gives you a fearless drive from within but also gives you the will to carry on when you need it most. It makes sense because if you're keeping everything charged regularly, the chances of having a blackout would be minimal to near impossible. Positive refuelling is often overlooked as unimportant in a modern-day society. It's one of those things that everyone thinks can be left out of the equation. And when things suddenly spark and go south, people have the audacity to ask how a mental decline happened.

When we sense something beginning to decline, that means we're aware. We're knowledgeable that one day, that thing will continue to plummet until we do something to change its course onto a better path. Sure, we could always leave it to someone else and not make an effort, but in the long run, you'll always wish you chose early intervention as opposed to chaotic strain in the future as we progress through life.

Why make it harder for ourselves later when we can make a few adjustments now?

Not bothering only comes back to have a negative impact on us later down the line.

50

IT'S OKAY IF YOU DON'T KNOW ALL THE ANSWERS

The manic speed of life weighs down on our shoulders, and we usually feel bad for getting something wrong. It's as though we've created a world where we penalise each other for not knowing all the answers to every situation. When stepping back to look at our society from the outside looking in, we realise how zoned out we've become in an age dominated by technology and social media.

What we should be doing is helping those around us to find the answers they seek in order to move forward. We rarely see enough of this happening in modern-day society. It's all too common to have a go at someone for messing something up. Nothing is gained if all you're doing is getting irate, but through working together as one to overcome the issue, we find the solution. Imagine what the world would be like if everyone acted in this manner.

Once we acknowledge what's actually happening around us, life becomes easier and far more manageable to digest. We might not know the answer to something today, but with the right amount of time spent learning about that subject, we are sure to discover the answer sooner or later. It's highly unlikely that anyone will ever know everything there is to learn because the universe is just too big.

There are so many species, so many plant variations, so many planets we're not even aware of. We've seen some of what Earth has to offer, but even then, we've barely scratched the surface. So how can someone claim to know all of the answers? It's impossible. And the way in which we see things through our own eyes might be seen in a more abstract definition by someone else. A good example of this is how we know about four seasons being the norm, but some areas of the world believe in five or six seasons because of the local conditions.

Keeping an open mind and a curious outlook on higher consciousness will teach us there is still clearly, a lot to absorb.

Some invigorating food for thought:

Are we using the full capacity and ability of our brains?

Could there be colours or senses we haven't witnessed before on other worlds?

If our solar system is part of a galaxy and there are hundreds of thousands more galaxies out there, surely there are other species living within them?

When we dream, could there be more meaning behind the occurrence, otherwise what significance would it serve?

Do we make full use of our senses to benefit us in our daily lives?

These are just some of the things we can contemplate in our spare time to instil confidence that it's okay if we don't know all the answers because nobody ever will.

> **Be an encourager... it'll benefit you more than being a pessimist. You'll become more intellectual too!**

51

EVERYONE HAS A ROLE

Believe it or not, we all have a part to play in life. No one is useless or incapable. Working consistently will eventually yield the results we're after and present new opportunities to us. When we're aiming for something specifically, we sometimes stumble into a new situation that forces us to level up.

We don't necessarily need to stand out in a way that brings us negative attention, but rather in a way that embraces who we are and what we're about. We always do better when we're not restricted to a black and white set of aims. A colouring book wasn't made to sit untouched, and your life is no different. It's a canvas waiting to be painted with your designs, ideas, and expressions.

Be fearless with your imagination in the world and don't be caged by other people's degree of living.

Be positive, build your confidence and don't wait around for a miracle to happen. You are the miracle, and the world needs your positive input to make it a greater place.

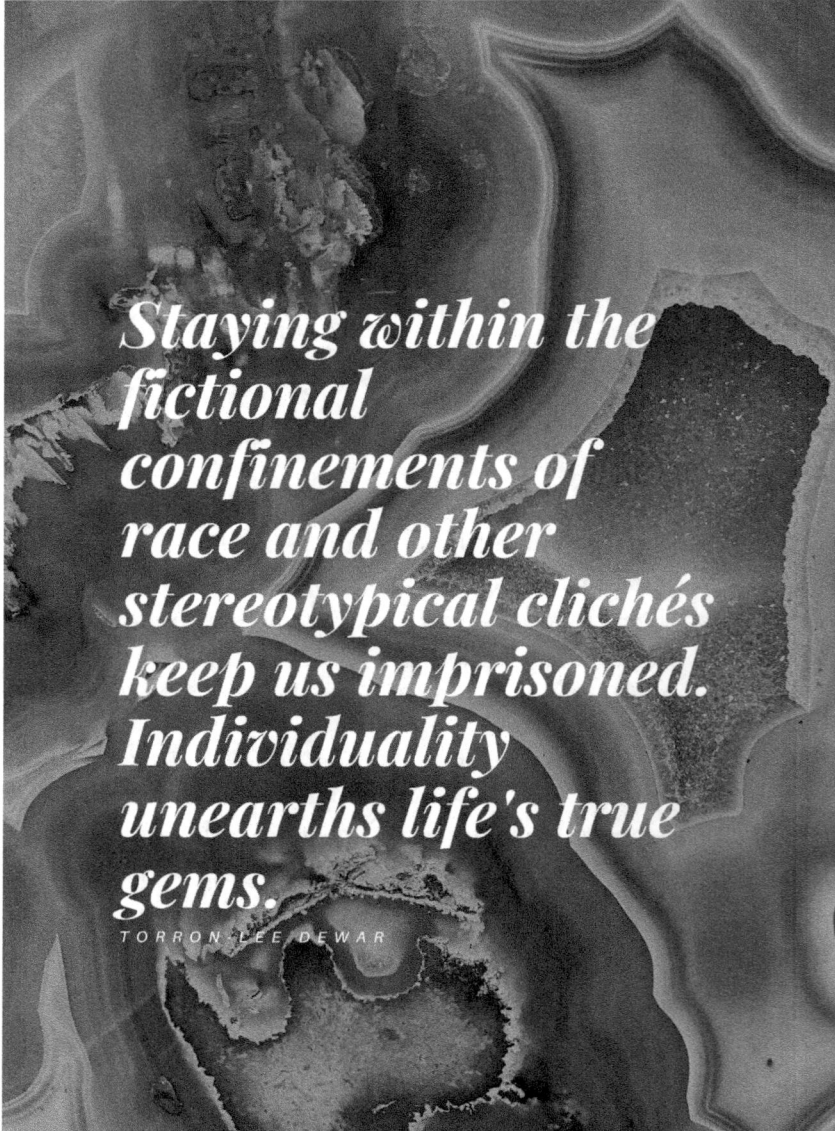

Staying within the fictional confinements of race and other stereotypical clichés keep us imprisoned. Individuality unearths life's true gems.

TORRON-LEE DEWAR

52

EVERYTHING YOU DO FROM NOW WILL DEFINE WHO YOU ARE

B e so busy working on your future that you forget the past. It's good to reminisce on the good old days from the previous years if it motivates you to move forward in a beneficial way.

But anything more than that will just slow you down and waste valuable time needed to shape your future. Cut the dead weight from your load so you can explore new things without unnecessary strain.

Start living the way you want from now. If you feel you can't do it from this very moment, then start working on plans to reach that aspiration. Just because you're not ready at this precise moment doesn't mean you should just mope around doing nothing. There's always something that you could get on with developing from this very moment. Or there might be things that can be prepared for when you are ready to implement any new additions to your life.

Start believing in your ambitions and let there be meaning behind your actions. We always have the option to change our egos and characters for the better. If you know you're doing things that are wrong, change your habits now before you do irreversible damage.

How many times have you heard someone say, "I'll do it some other time?" That's a forbidden way of thinking that needs to be avoided as much as possible! Actions always speak louder than words and it's better to be a doer than a talker. Making more moves on life's chessboard will strengthen your ability to deliver whilst flourishing your creative drive in the process. It really is all about enjoying the adventure and the struggle... building that endurance up until you're roughly where you want to be.

53

CREATIVE FLOWCHARTS

Coming up with a unique idea can be confusing at times if we don't really know where to start. Going back to what we discussed earlier about being your own type of character, these charts should help you grasp the confidence to move forward. Simplicity is often the key to solving our problems.

It can be hard to break away from the herd and do the things you've always wanted to do. The first step to leadership is getting on with just that... leading the way!

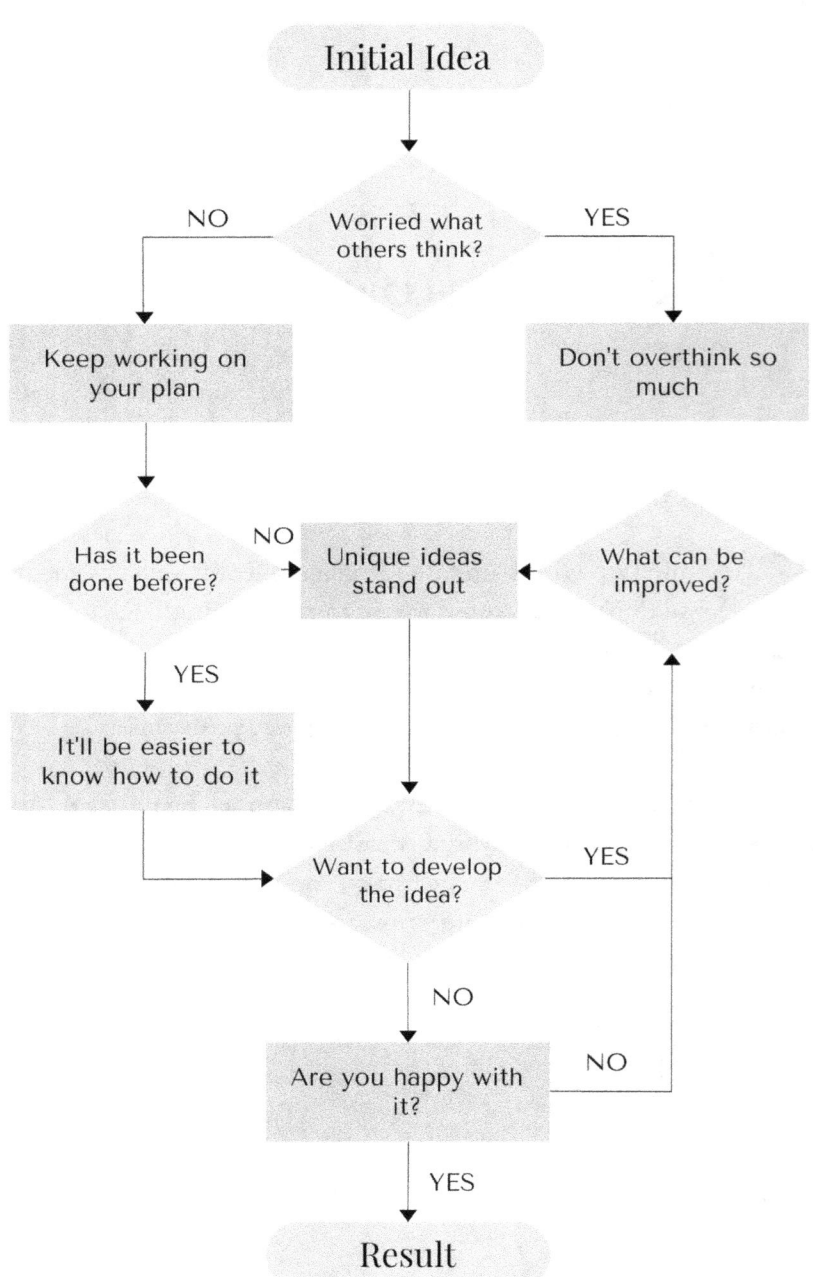

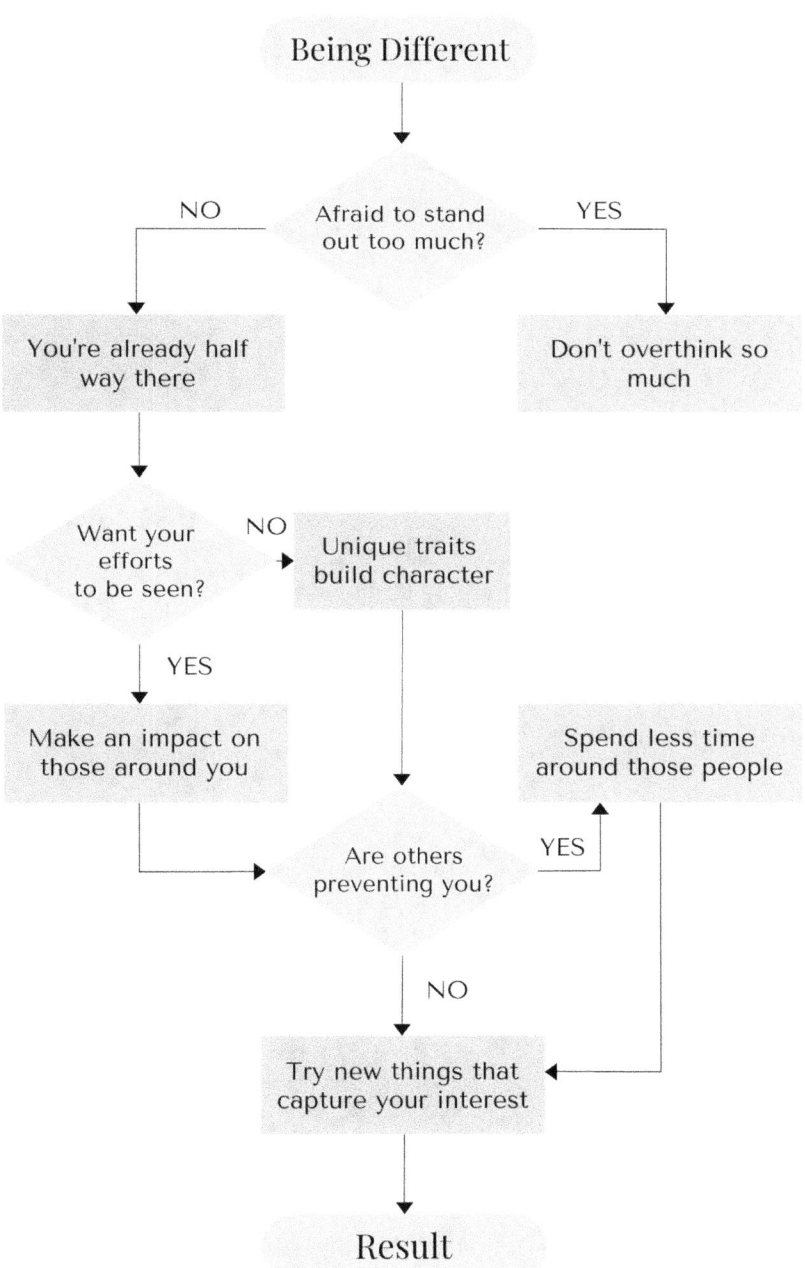

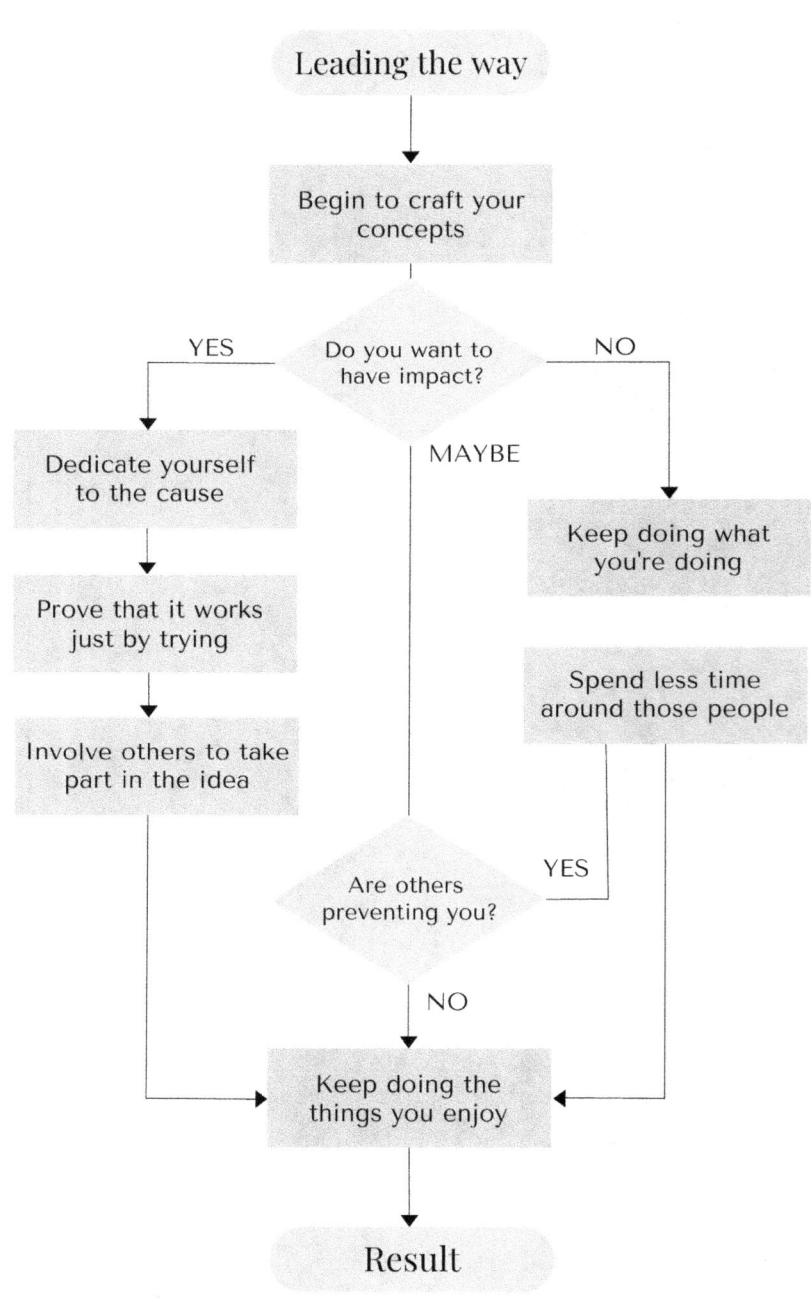

54

IT'S OKAY TO SWITCH PATHS

There have been many times I've switched paths throughout the course of life. Each time, re-emerging as a better version of myself. There was a rough concept in my mind of what I wanted to achieve, and I worked on constructing a business during the final years of school. I went to college to do mechanics but still didn't really know what I wanted out of life.

I guess it was purely because I hadn't been out in the field enough to know. That's the problem with career choices and work experience... it's quite limited. You must seek opportunities out yourself and build up from there. After attending college for some time, I got to know how certain things worked. But it wasn't long before I was unhappy with myself... wondering what it would be like to keep working on my business ideas.

I dropped out of the course in the end to pursue my own ventures. It felt like it was a risk, but at the same time, it was a relief to finally be able to get on with what I wanted to do. I always told myself, if I work hard enough at it, I wouldn't need to worry so much about a so-called backup plan. People wasted more time sorting out their plan B than they spent working on their plan A. It was precious time wasted. I just wanted to see what else was out there before committing to the system and being put on a 9-5 job. In those years, I tried new things that would push my current set of skills, all while working at different jobs that I didn't like. I already had 5 years of artistic experience behind me, so I knew I could do that. It's always a good idea to start with either something you're interested in or something you're good at.

I opened up classes of my own aimed at performing artists and the ball began to roll. New people started to join and as the years passed, I made them part of our staff once they understood the ethos. That initial "idea" developed and became a registered charity, winning numerous awards for its community reach and ability to bring people together.

I had to work harder than I've ever worked in my life to get it there, but it was more than worth it. The process taught me so many things that weren't even related to the arts such as work leadership, finance management, workspace ideas, and lots more. Being an entrepreneur forced me to stand up for my aims with my head held high. Dealing with setbacks, stressful barriers, and negativity from others whilst maintaining a positive outlook makes you a mentally strong person. I thought that by quitting college, I was failing when really, I was throwing myself in the deep end of opportunity.

As you progress through life you'll realise that the sooner you embrace your own wishes, the sooner you'll be on your way to living a happier lifestyle. We weren't made to live life in an entrapment following a set of basic rules that someone drafted up for us.

As long as our plans involve bettering ourselves positively, what is there to really worry about?

55

AGE ISN'T AN EXCUSE FOR NOT TRYING

Being a certain age should by no means become a barrier that stops us from achieving what we want. We're always blinded by the hearsay of society. Things like "You're too young to start thinking this way" or "You're too old to chase your desires" are all too commonly heard. Being young isn't something to be ashamed of and being old doesn't mean life can't be lived to the fullest. Age is something that holds many of us back, taking up a lot of time and capacity within our brains as to what we should and shouldn't be doing.

When it comes to the fulfilment of our goals, we must forget that age even exists. It only shows how long we've been roaming the planet for and nothing else. As we age, we should aim to improve in some way every year. There's a lot to be getting on with and a lot to learn about. Being held back by imaginary barriers isn't the way to get ahead. Getting on with what you want to do and making the most of your time is what you need to be fixated on.

Instead of being anxious about being too young or getting older, learn to embrace the years with pride and be a motivator to all of those who are a similar age to you. Great minds come in all shapes and sizes. Going back to what I said before, we're never one thing but rather, many all at once.

We shouldn't view ourselves as just a number, colour, or any other one thing. When we do that, we're holding ourselves back mentally. So just be yourself and refrain from living in a box.

56

UNEXPECTED ALLIES

Friendships usually form when we're around others of similar traits, for example, school or work. Sometimes, friendships happen between people with totally opposite backgrounds for a variety of reasons. The most likely reason is that they find inspiration in each other's endeavours, whilst appreciating the company of their contrasting nature. A certain warmth or motivation can spark between our human characters and perhaps one can offer the advice or reassurance the other couldn't find from someone of their own age or background.

It's unwise to think that the appearance of a person can determine what they can or can't provide us in terms of achievable happiness or impactful insight. Always give someone a chance to show themselves before dismissing them because of where they're from or how they were brought up.

I always found that the unpopular, quieter people in school were often the ones with the best personalities that you could have an in-depth conversation with. You could always learn a thing or two from these people whereas the loudmouths never had anything of value to offer in terms of knowledge. They were good at all things sport but that was pretty much where it ended. Most of the time, favoured people in school were popular for all the wrong reasons.

My neighbour that used to live above me was a lady that had survived WWII named Doreen. My family knew her and her partner Ted since my great-grandmother was around, and I was always inspired by the stories she would share about her upbringing. When someone from a different era gives you an insight into what times were like, it really does make you grateful towards the position you're currently in.

Doreen would tell me about having to travel across Kew by boat when the Thames flooded so she could reach the doctor and have the cut on her head treated which happened in the blast. I'd sit there drinking either a cup of tea or a glass of Vimto whilst picturing what it would've been like at the time. Time would go so fast during our conversations, as I was always so intrigued, taking so much on board. Before you knew it, the street lamps would be pinging on outside. Back then, they turned a sort of reddish colour before turning to the yellowy ambience we all know. That's when it would be time to go back downstairs. Being told about the war and times passed is one thing, but actually hearing it from someone via their real life experiences is truly moving. You sort of begin to paint a picture of what that person would be going through at the time and how they would overcome a certain issue being posed upon them.

Another interesting thing about Doreen was her sense of overall pride in everything she did. From her mauve rinse permed hair to the cleanliness of her home. There would be classic things like the old-fashioned globe-shaped Hoover out in the hall still going strong from what I presume was the 50s or 60s and a wooden clock that you had to put a key in to wind. All of these bygone things sparked curiosity, as no one else I knew had these procedures.

As time came upon us, I took the Olympic torch over to Doreen's so she could marvel at its grandness even though I no longer lived in the flats. She couldn't really see it because her vision had deteriorated, but I passed it to her and explained what it looked like in appearance with its shimmering gold exterior and 8,000 holes that resembled each torchbearer. She kept on smiling the entire time and I could tell that it made her evening.

I took a picture of her holding it, got it printed, and signed the back with a marker pen. When I handed it across to her, she got out the magnifying glass with a light on it, looked at the image of herself, and read what I wrote. The smile she made was priceless.

Reminiscing on the good old days, it's clear that somehow, our friendship helped to sculpt part of who I am today. Values are built upon by spending extra time around good people, which in turn leads to an upgraded personality. The Internet cannot teach you everything. Some things can only be learned through genuine energy being transferred, being met with face-to-face experiences.

Too frequently, our time is spent trying to get in with the wrong crowd, and before you know it, we've wasted years of our valuable energy. As my Nan always said, the earlier you realise it's not worth entertaining false friendships, the quicker you'll grow as a person.

These are all prime examples of how we're able to help and learn from one another no matter who we are or what we look like. There will always be something you don't know or haven't heard of that someone can teach you. From this, we apply the knowledge to our own everyday lives so we can seize every opportunity and be humble for what we already have.

Absorbing useful information from others is what upgrades us. Being able to apply something from somewhere else to improve our own plans is being creatively resourceful.

57

WHAT YOU SEE IS WHAT YOU GET

What happens when we intake something that doesn't agree with us? We get sick so the body can rid itself of the toxins causing the malfunction. But what happens when we see or watch things that we didn't necessarily want to see? The brain harbours the thoughts, processing them over and over again until we ourselves are infected mentally. Our brains cannot eliminate what they've already been fed that easily, which is why it's so important to see more of the things that uplift you.

Tying in with the earlier chapter about not becoming someone you don't want to be, this is one of the most important. When the brain is constantly filled with bad things, it won't be long until you're blindsided by the many visions of madness. Have you ever watched something terrible and wish you could unsee it? Sticking to the saner things on television means you're not constantly replaying weird scenarios in your head. "It's only fiction," you say, "It can't possibly have an effect on us." The truth is, it does. It doesn't matter if what we see is fictitious or non-fictitious, our eyes still see the situation, and the subconscious brain still digests the situation as it is.

For example, watching horror movie after horror movie will only make you suffer from paranoia in the long run. People like to think they're being brave by trying or doing things that aren't good for the mind. All they're doing is setting themselves up for a later fate somewhere down the line. It might seem trivial, but do not underestimate what harmful sights can do to your own visions.

If you know a certain series has horrible episodes, simply stop watching it. The constant trauma is wreaking havoc on the brain, which doesn't understand why it's seeing these things constantly. Modern media tricks us into coming back for more so we can see what the outcome was. The terrible thing about that is, some storylines never see a positive outcome and that is part of the trickery to keep you coming back to this woeful circle of gloom.

Our actions today have consequences tomorrow and it's always good to bear that in mind. Just because what you're witnessing isn't something of your own doing, it doesn't mean that your brain isn't trying to adapt to what's going on. We are forever evolving as humans. What you see either pushes your mind to greater intent or halts its positive progression toxically. Everything you're doing is shaping the type of person you are. Why would you fill your mind with madness if that were not something you'd want for your own life? Just like our diet, tiny quantities of hazardous foods ingested can go unnoticed... keep ingesting the bad things and it won't be long before your health declines.

If you wanted the plants in your garden to grow strong and show their full potential, you'd use water on them. You wouldn't use bleach, so why do it to your brain? Nourish it more often.

Rule of thumb: Stick to witnessing more positives over negatives, so you can function without the fog of insanity looming over your head.

58

FIND HUMOUR IN EVERY SCENARIO

Finding humour in every dull scenario makes things better. If you're ever in a situation when you feel stressed or on the verge of depression, think about something funny. Keep replaying comedic thoughts in your mind until your worries disappear.

Sometimes in life, we just have to laugh at our own misfortune. Seeing the bright side means that we've accepted our circumstances and are willing to proceed with confidence. Being able to move forward from unfortunate events starts with a clear, undoubted mind.

Finding humour in your own setbacks doesn't mean you're disrespecting yourself. It means that you're unbothered by the impact it had on you. With humour there to uplift our spirits, we can get through anything. Life is unpredictable, and when it weighs down the positivity scale, having a good laugh restores the balance. Use it more frequently. It's certainly there for a reason.

Lighten up and see the funny side of life when you feel the blues approaching. Don't take everything so seriously.

59

IDEAS DEVELOP UNEXPECTEDLY

All of the best ideas always seem to fall upon us when we're trying to tune out from the world. Usually when we're laying in bed striving to get some rest. In fact, the majority of thoughts that sculpted this very book were created at night when striving to get some shut-eye. This goes to show how powerful the mind becomes when we're winding down for the day. All of our greatest thoughts and ideologies ignite because we have nothing but time to let them dance.

Everything becomes so vivid and aligned when silence surrounds us in a dark environment. Our imagination can strike the hardest at these times because our brains aren't as polluted with the stress of everything else going on throughout the day. Always make a note of those brainwaves that solve your problems or challenge you, so you're able to refer back to them the day after. A small notepad under your bed or tucked away in your bedside table will be of good use. This will allow you to improve on whatever you were thinking about during the night, so you can turn those brainwaves into sustainable outcomes.

In these moments, it's as if the mind tells us where to look and where to locate the answers to our problems. These powerful moments of thought can sometimes be like finding the missing pieces to the puzzle. So start by acknowledging these signs and following up on those constructive concepts. Not all of our problem-solving takes place in the daytime so understand how better quality concepts appear when the stars are out!

Like anything in life, don't overdo it. Accept when it's time to switch off.

60

NO ONE IS INTIMIDATING

One of the most important things to always bear in mind is that not everyone is as powerful and clued up, as they appear to be. People hide behind acts they must keep in motion every day and wear masks to hide their own insecurities. It secretly weighs them down heavily, but they'll never tell you that. When striving for success, it may seem as though people misjudge your true worth, standing ignorant to what you're actually capable of. Those that make your path difficult to navigate all started with a dream and the desire to fulfil it. This means that you stand a chance as much as the next person, and your success will sometimes depend on how much you want to prove narrow-minded people wrong.

We need to use the pessimism of others as motivation to come out on top. When someone doubts our abilities, it should make us work even harder to better ourselves. Thinking quietly the whole time with the words of "You may laugh and judge me now, but sooner or later you will notice me" often alleviates the stress of demanding, demotivational people. Some people can never be pleased, and all we're doing is running a marathon that has no finish line. Refrain from entering a race of condescending decline with no value.

It's intensely rewarding to feel the impact of surprise from negative people when they realise the lengths you went to in order to succeed. If we keep fighting the good fight and continue to work productively, it won't be long before we reap the rewards of perseverance and the critics have no choice but to take us seriously.

Regardless of all of the above, we aren't out to please others. That's just something that does or doesn't happen in the process. When it's all said and done, it really doesn't matter if someone doesn't notice you. You notice yourself.

In some form eventually, you get back what you put in.

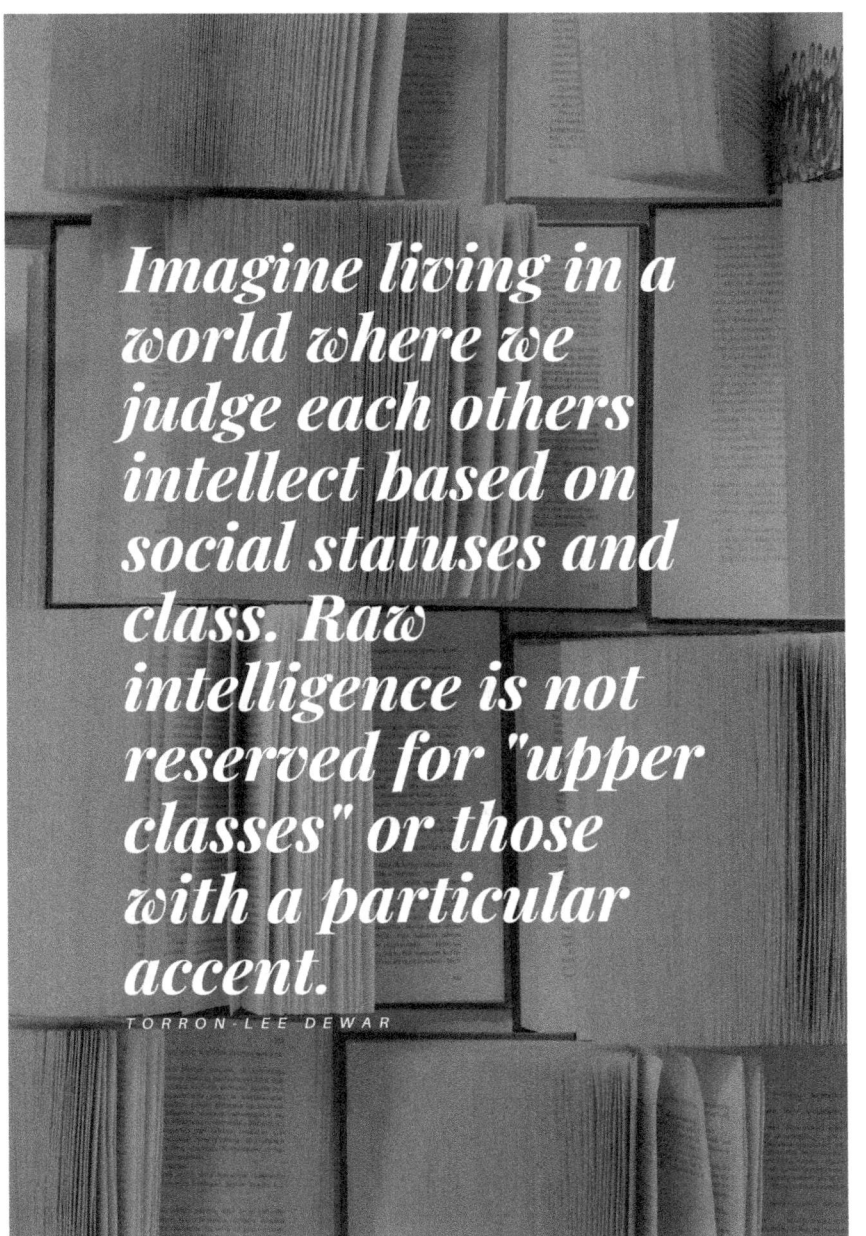

Imagine living in a world where we judge each others intellect based on social statuses and class. Raw intelligence is not reserved for "upper classes" or those with a particular accent.

TORRON-LEE DEWAR

61

ABSOLUTE CERTAINTY

You might not think you have the knowledge to accomplish something on a large scale, but you do. People aren't told that enough.

It's really all about not giving up and being so determined that it's impossible to fail. What others consider unsuccessful might be everything you've wanted in terms of success. But you don't do it for the doubters. You do it because you have ideas you want to grow, and energies you wish to maximise. It's never too late to change the path that you're on if you're not satisfied. The sooner you get on with what you need to be doing, the better. Whether that's travelling more, doing more of what makes you happy, being around those who bring you peace or just painting that fence you've been talking about for ages, the time is now.

Avoid the pitfalls of constantly sacrificing your own happiness. Time is slowly passing each week, and there is so much goodness to be extracted from each day if we allow it. Break so-called toxic traditions, try new things and above all, appreciate who you are and what you stand for. There's absolutely no need to put your happiness on hold. Radiate your good desires more often. Instead of blending in all the time, learn to lead the pack with your own visions. Start trends, support others, and be a decent human being. Surround yourself with positive people who make you feel good about being yourself. Life's too short to mess around doing anything else.

It's okay to try and fail. In fact, you have to fail a few times to know how to do it right. Because we live in fear of not wanting to be humiliated, we prevent ourselves from trying new things that allow us to reach our highest creative potential. Even those who pretend to make all of the right decisions leading to success fell flat on their face at some stage. They just didn't broadcast their progress for you to see that happen.

Feel like you've done well or overcome a certain challenging obstacle? Reward yourself. We're far too harsh on ourselves when it comes to self-appreciation and acceptance of who we are. After all, we're human and life is what you make it with little improvements being made each day. Feeling good about ourselves for no reason whatsoever is a healthy trait to foster. If we can train ourselves to do that, everything flows flawlessly. It's a defensive mechanism that deflects bad energy away from us so we can proceed to the next day with minimal doubt.

If you already have imaginative ideas that give you a buzz, keep working on them. Develop something that reflects your character, as that's what being creative is all about. We really can achieve anything, it just depends on how determined we are. Steer clear of those who always say and never do. Others will find ways to put you down and make life difficult. Succeed anyway and be creatively empowered in all walks of life.

As you embark on a new journey acquiring your enhanced mindset, how are you going to embrace your inner creativity?

Let your mind be as big as the universe. Infinite.

TORRON-LEE DEWAR

www.ingramcontent.com/pod-product-compliance
Lightning Source LLC
Chambersburg PA
CBHW062201280526
45788CB00001B/388